# DIANA LEVINE KNITS
# CIRCULAR KNITTING MACHINE PATTERNS

**Contact:**
dianalevineknits.com
instagram.com/dianalevineknits

D1663375

# TABLE OF CONTENTS

# The Techniques

# The Templates

# THE PATTERNS

**32** MESSENGER BAG PURSES

**34** GEOMETRIC BAGS

**38** STRIPED BAGS

**40** BALLERINA DOLL

**44** TOTE BAGS

**48** LARGE TOTE BAGS

**52** BOW HEADBANDS

**56** WRISTLET CLUTCH

**60** I-CORD BRACELETS

**62** SHOULDER BAG

**64** CROSS BODY PHONEBAG

**68** WIDE GEOMETRIC BAGS

**72** PENCIL CASES

**74** FLOWER BOUQUET

**78** FLOWER HEADBANDS

**80** MINI PURSES

**84** RAINBOW HAT

**86** THROW PILLOW

**88** CHECKERED BLANKET

**92** BOAT TOTE

**96** TRAVEL BAG

**100** TRIANGLE BAG

**102** DESIGN-YOUR-OWN HAT ACTIVITY

**104** DESIGN-YOUR-OWN SCARF ACTIVITY

**106** RAINBOW FINGERLESS GLOVES

# WELCOME!

In this volume of *Circular Knitting Machine Patterns*, you'll find patterns for bags, hats, headbands, home accessories, and more—knit with 4, 22, 40, 46 and 48 needle circular knitting machines!

Dear reader,

Thank you so much for reading *Circular Knitting Machine Patterns,* featuring 25 projects to make using 4, 22, 40, 46 and 48 needle circular knitting machines.

Circular knitting machines have brought so much joy to my life, and with this book, I hope to share that joy with you.

With circular knitting machines, you can make a wide variety of projects: from hats and headbands, to bags, pillows, blankets, home decor and more.

I first learned how to knit as a child—and knitting has been an important part of my life throughout my childhood, teen years, during college and beyond.

And then—during the winter of 2020-2021, I discovered circular knitting machines! It truly felt like magic to realize that I could knit up so many beautiful projects—so quickly! One of my favorite parts of knitting is creating custom-made, unique gifts for my family and friends—made with love. However, as a busy Mom, balancing parenthood and work, it's challenging to find time to hand-knit gifts for friends and family. Creating projects with circular knitting machines speeds up the knitting process so that I can create custom gifts for so many of the people that I love.

In this book, you'll find an introduction to some of the circular knitting machines available on the market, followed by a section on techniques, introducing some of the basic concepts of working with circular knitting machines—casting on and off, seaming the pieces, how to assemble a hat, as well some of my favorite tips and tricks for working with these machines.

In the pattern section, you'll find a variety of projects to create, including bags, a blanket, a doll, a few hats and headbands, a pillow, and more—I hope that the next time you're looking for inspiration for your next project, you'll flip through these pages and find something that will inspire creativity.

And the last section of the book features some blank templates for some of the projects in the book, for you to sketch out and plan for your own designs.

I want to give a warm thank you to the people who have supported my crafty journey along the way. To the people who have viewed my YouTube channel, connected with me on Instagram, Facebook, TikTok or Pinterest—and to the readers who have purchased my books—thank you. It is a joy to design these projects and patterns to share with you, and every kind message of support is so meaningful to me, and inspires me to keep designing. Becoming part of the knitting machine community has been such a wonderful part of discovering this craft. Many of the patterns in this book are easily customizable. From choosing different color combinations, to adding a variety of decorations or details, there are so many ways to put your own spin on these patterns.

If you enjoy this book, you may also like the second volume—*Circular Knitting Machine Patterns Vol. 2,* featuring 25 projects to make using 4, 22, 46 and 48 needle circular knitting machines. The second volume includes patterns for holiday decorations for Christmas and Halloween, pillows, bags, a stuffed animal, and more. You can find the book on Amazon, or at dianalevineknits.com.

If you make any of the projects in this book, please share them with me! You can find me on social media: @dianalevineknits on Instagram, Facebook, YouTube, Pinterest, TikTok and Etsy.

With gratitude,
Diana

# MEET THE MACHINES!

A quick introduction to some of the common circular knitting machines on the market. In my patterns, I refer to them as 22 needle, 40 needle, 46 needle, 48 needle knitting machines, and I-Cord knitting machines.

There are numerous brands and sizes of circular knitting machines. When first learning about circular knitting machines, it can be confusing because there are so many to choose from! I'll share a quick introduction to some of the machines I use in my knitting studio—however, please keep in mind that this is just a selection of what's available in 2021, and is *not* an exhaustive list. There are other brands and sizes available, and more options may come onto the market over time.

## 48 NEEDLE SENTRO™

The 48 needle Sentro™ knitting machine is a knitting machine commonly used to make hats. This machine comes with both a row counter and a tensioner with 3 options, which provides tension to the yarn without having to hold the yarn in your hand.

*48 needle Sentro™ knitting machine*

## 46 NEEDLE ADDI® EXPRESS KINGSIZE

This is the large size Addi® Express Kingsize circular knitting machine, which features 46 needles. It is often used to make hats, scarves, purses and large stuffed animals. The machine comes with a counter, but does not come with a tensioner. With the Addi® Express knitting machines, you can change the tension in the yarn by how tightly you hold the yarn. There are two options when using all of these knitting machines—circular or panel knitting. All of the projects in this book are knit with the circular setting.

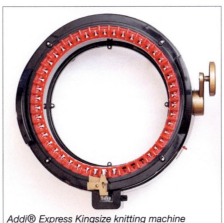

*Addi® Express Kingsize knitting machine*

## 40 NEEDLE SENTRO™

There are a number of 40 needle circular knitting machines on the market, including the Sentro™ 40 needle knitting machine. A similar model is also sold under the brand name Jamit™. This machine is like the 48 needle Sentro™, except that it has 40 needles (instead of 48). And notably, it does not come with a row counter attached to the machine. So if you use this machine, I suggest purchasing a row counter separately. Or, you can always keep track of row counts using paper and pen. The 40 needle machines are often used to make twisted headbands, scarves, bags, and baby hats. Please note that 40 needle knitting machines are too small to make adult sized hats.

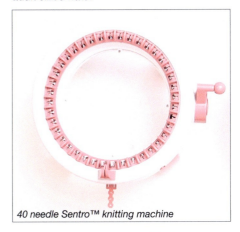

*40 needle Sentro™ knitting machine*

Some projects commonly knit with a 46 or 48 needle circular knitting machine include hats, headbands, twisted headbands, dolls or stuffed animals, and larger bags.

Some projects commonly knit with a 40 needle circular knitting machine include headbands and twisted headbands. A circular knit piece from a 40 needle knitting machine will be narrower than a circular knit piece from a 46 needle machine.

# MEET THE MACHINES ...CONTINUED

### 40 NEEDLE KNIT QUICK™ LOOPS & THREADS® MACHINE

The Knit Quick™ by Loops & Threads® is a 40 needle circular knitting machine. This machine comes with a tensioner to hold the yarn—but does not come with a row counter. So, you'll need to either purchase a separate row counter, or keep count with pen and paper.

*40 needle Knit Quick™ from Loops & Threads®*

### 22 NEEDLE ADDI® EXPRESS PROFESSIONAL KNITTING MACHINE

The Addi® Express 22 needle knitting machine produces a piece of circular knitting approximately 3" wide. With this machine, you can knit 3" headbands, small dolls, and purses. You can also use the 22 needle machine to knit small blankets, among other projects. Like the Addi® Express Kingsize, the 22 needle Addi® does come with a row counter, but does not come with a tensioner. So you can control the tension of the yarn by how tightly you hold the yarn.

*22 needle Addi® Express Professional machine*

### 4-6 NEEDLE I-CORD KNITTING MACHINES

An I-Cord knitting machine is a 4 to 6 needle circular knitting machine. There are numerous brands on the market. The knitter shown here is the Tulip™ I-Cord knitter. There's also the Prym™, the Embellish-Knit™. There is also the Addi® Egg, which features 6 needles. These machines quickly knit I-Cords. However, if you don't have one of these machines, you can easily hand-knit an I-Cord using two double pointed knitting needles.

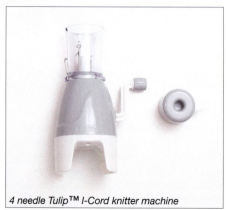

*4 needle Tulip™ I-Cord knitter machine*

### "WHICH MACHINE SHOULD I BUY?"

People often ask me "which knitting machine should I buy?" And the answer always is: "it depends!" It depends on the type of projects you want to knit, your budget, and your personal preference for which brand circular knitting machine you like working with best. In terms of which machines work best for which projects, I would personally (and this is a *personal opinion*!) suggest the following:

• **Adult sized Hats:** Addi® Express Kingsize 46 needle knitting machine or Sentro™ 48 needle
• **Twisted headbands:** Sentro™ 40 needle, KnitQuick™ 40 needle machine or Addi® Express Kingsize knitting machine
• **Scarves:** Addi® Express 46 needle Kingsize knitting machine, Sentro™ 40, KnitQuick™ 40 needle machine, or Sentro™ 48 needle.
• **Blankets:** Addi® Express 46 needle Kingsize knitting machine or Sentro™ 48 needle knitting machine
• **Purses and bags:** Addi® Express 46 needle Kingsize knitting machine, Sentro™ 48 needle knitting machine, or for small/medium bags, Addi® Express Professional 22 needle knitting machine.
• **Small headbands:** Addi® Express Professional 22 needle knitting machine.

### VINTAGE KNITTING MACHINES

The machines shown on these pages are all current knitting machines (purchased in 2021). However, there are vintage circular knitting machines around as well—they can sometimes be found at second-hand shops or online.

## FLAT BED KNITTING MACHINES

In this book, I refer to "knitting machines", and for the purposes of this book, I'm always referring specifically to *circular* knitting machines. That being said, the term "knitting machines" encompasses not just circulars, but flatbed knitting machines as well.

## KNITTING TAGS

The knitting tags featured in this book were custom-made by *Archer Knits*. You can order the tags at archerknits.com.

## YARN

You can use a variety of yarns with circular knitting machines—however, weight 3 or 4 yarns tend to work best. All of the projects in this book were made using Loops & Threads® Impeccable™ yarn (a Weight 4/ Medium yarn) in a variety of colors.

If you try a yarn and it doesn't work well with your machine, don't give up. Some people find certain brands or styles of yarn work better on their machines than others. Please refer to the manual that came with your machine for specific advice to which weight and style yarns the manufacturer suggests will work best with that particular knitting machine.

## PATTERN REFERENCES

In my books, I refer to the circular knitting machines by their number of needles. Here are the machines I'm referring to, broken down by number of needles.

**4 needle I-Cord knitting machines**
4 needle I-Cord knitting machines, such as the Tulip™ I-Cord knitter machine.

**22 needle knitting machines**
This refers to knitting machines such as the 22 needle Addi® Express Professional knitting machine, Sentro™ 22 needle knitting machine, or Jamit™ 22 needle knitting machine.

**40 needle knitting machines**
This refers to knitting machines such as the 40 needle Sentro™ knitting machine, the 40 needle Jamit™ knitting machine, or the 40 needle Loops & Threads® Knit Quick™ knitting machine.

**46 needle knitting machine**
This refers to the 46 needle Addi® Express Kingsize knitting machine.

**48 needle knitting machine**
This refers to the 48 needle Sentro™ knitting machine or the 48 needle Jamit™ knitting machine.

**Note:** Since this book was published, there may be new machines on the market, and/or some of these knitting machines may no longer be available. These machines shown on these pages were available in 2021.

For the most current, up to date information on which knitting machines are available, I suggest joining a local or online knitting machine group and asking around for suggestions for which knitting machine may work best for you. Or, you may want to try reaching out to your local yarn store and ask for advice. There are also many videos online reviewing and showing some of the knitting machines available.

*Knit with a 22 needle circular knitting machine*

*Knit with a 46 or 48 needle knitting machine*

*Knit with a 40 needle knitting machine*

# The Techniques

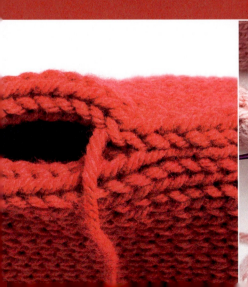

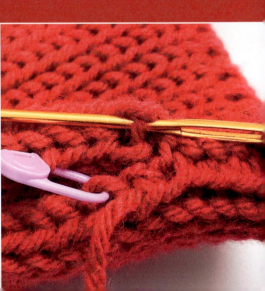

# Casting On and Off with Scrap Yarn

This is one of the two main methods of casting on and off of a circular knitting machine. By using scrap yarn, you keep the stitches "live" for you to seam when finishing your project.

When knitting hats, dolls, and any projects where you will "cinch" a side of the work, you'll cast on and off directly with the yarn you're using for the project. However, for many projects, including scarves, headbands, and purses—you'll need to cast on and off using a **scrap yarn**.

**Scrap yarn** is a length of yarn that you'll be removing at the end of the project, so the color you choose doesn't matter to how the project will look in the end. The most important part of the color choice is making sure that it **contrasts well** with your main color, which will make it easier to see the stitches when you're seaming.

### FIND THE FIRST NEEDLE
Locate the first contrasting needle on your machine. On the Addi®, it will be the first black needle. On the Sentro™, it will be the only black or only white needle.

### CAST ON ROW
Using your scrap yarn (the yarn you'll be removing at the end of the project), wrap the yarn around the first needle with the yarn tail in the center. Leave a 5 or 6" tail in the yarn.

Then, using the working yarn (not the yarn tail), turn the knob slowly and wrap the yarn around the **back of the second needle** and then in **front of the third needle**.

Continue in this process, wrapping the yarn back and forth along all the needles, until you reach the first needle again. Before you reach the needle where you first wrapped your scrap yarn, wrap the yarn behind the needle to it's right, and place the yarn into the yarn holder.

If you're working with an Addi®, close the yarn holder. If you're working with a Sentro™, place it into the yarn holder and then place the yarn into the tensioner.

### SCRAP YARN CAST ON
You just finished your cast on row. Set your counter back to zero. Rotate the knob and continue knitting until you reach the first needle again.

When you reach the first needle again, you've just completed your first row of knitting. Knit another row.

If you're using an Addi®, **hold the yarn in your left hand to provide tension.** You just finished the second row of knitting. You'll see half of the needles have the yarn wrapped around the needles, and half do not. This is normal for the second row.

Knit another row—after the third row, there should now be stitches around every needle. Knit two more rows, for a total of 5 scrap yarn rows. **You can knit anywhere from 5 to 10 rows for the scrap yarn,** but 5 is the minimum.

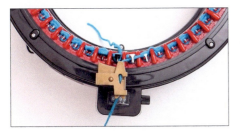

When you finish 5 rows of the scrap yarn, cut a 5 or 6" tail in the scrap yarn.

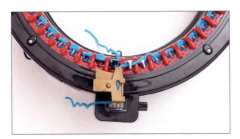

Open the yarn holder (if you're using an Addi®), and throw the yarn tail in the middle of the machine, to the right side of the first needle where you cast on earlier.

### SWITCHING TO THE MAIN COLOR YARN

Next, we'll switch to the **main color yarn** (the yarn you want to use for your project). For some projects, you'll only need to leave a 5 or 6" tail. For other projects, where you'll need to use the yarn tail for seaming, you'll need to leave a very long yarn tail.

Place the new (main color) yarn into the yarn holder, where your scrap yarn was placed earlier. Place the main color yarn tail in the center of the machine, **together with the scrap yarn tail** (to the right of the needle where you first cast on).

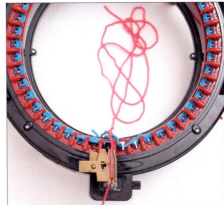

If you're using an Addi®, close the holder.

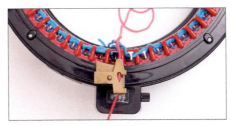

Hold the two yarn tails together. Slowly turn the knob to knit the first few stitches and then pause. After you've knit a few stitches, turn your counter back to zero.

Continue knitting until you reach the first needle again. You've just completed your first row of main color knitting.

After 10 rows, this is how your knitting will look:

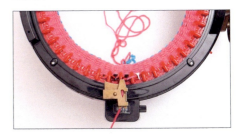

After 20 rows, this is how your knitting will look:

# CASTING ON AND OFF WITH SCRAP YARN ...Continued

For this example, we'll finish the project at 20 rows of the main color. (This would be an example of how you'd knit a **scrunchie**). Next, cut a yarn tail in the main color yarn (leaving a longer tail if you'll need to use the yarn to seam the project later), and throw it in the middle of the machine, **to the right of the needle where you first cast on.**

## SCRAP YARN CAST OFF
Next, switch back to the scrap yarn color. Place the yarn tail (5 or 6" is fine) in the middle of the machine, **together with the main color yarn tail, to the right of the needle where you first cast on.**

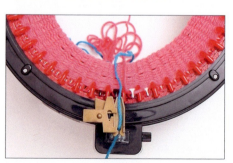

Close the yarn holder (if using an Addi®) and hold the two tails together, close and low, as you slowly knit the next row.

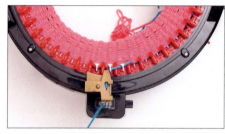

After a few stitches, set your counter back to zero. Continue knitting until the end of the row.

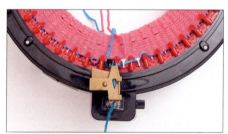

You just finished your first row of the scrap yarn cast off. Continue knitting until you reach **at least 5 rows.**

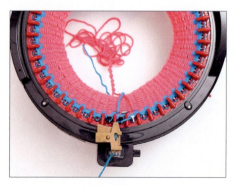

## CASTING OFF
When you reach 5 rows of the scrap yarn, cut a short tail in the scrap yarn.

After the scrap yarn is cut, continue turning the knob until the work falls off the needles.

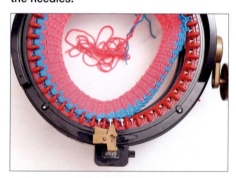

If the work gets stuck on the last couple of needles, pull them off manually. After your works falls off, your piece is finished and ready to be seamed!

# Tips & Tricks

These are some of my favorite tips and tricks for working with circular knitting machines. There can be a learning curve when first working with circular knitting machines, and I hope these tips will help make the process easier.

## SECURING YOUR MACHINES

It's very important when working with circular knitting machines that you securely attach your machine to your working surface. If you're working with an Addi™ machine, use the clamps provided with the machine to securely attach the machine to the table.

If the bottom of the clamps are sharp and are hurting your legs when you're knitting, you can cover the bottom of the clamps with a piece of gaff tape, or other soft material, to prevent the clamps from poking your legs.

When I work with Sentro™ or Jamit™ circular knitting machines, I use velcro dots to attach the machine to the table. These also make it very easy to remove and re-attach the machine.

## EXPERIMENTING WITH DIFFERENT YARN

When I have a friend who is purchasing their first circular knitting machine, I remind them **not to stock up on a ton of yarn for their machine, until after they've tried out the yarn**. Depending on the yarn, your machine, and even the humidity in your room, some machines, in certain environments, work "better" with some yarns than others.

The best way to find out which yarns work well with your machine is to try them out! So when you first purchase your machine, I'd suggest buying a few different types of yarn, trying one project with each, and getting a feel for which works well with your machine. It's a different process than when choosing a yarn for a hand-knit or hand-crocheted project. It's not just about the color and weight—there are other factors that could make a yarn more or less difficult to work with in your particular circular knitting machine. So, before you

stock up on dozens of skeins of yarn for your machine, purchase one skein, try it out and see what you think!

## KEEP TRYING

The first time I used a circular knitting machine, the teeny-tiny hat that I knit was uneven, bumpy, and the stitches were not consistent. If I had let myself give up then, I would never have known the joy of creating beautiful, professional looking pieces of knitwear with my circular knitting machines. It takes time to get the hang of using these machines, and it's normal for it to take some experimenting. If you have questions, join a circular knitting machine group—you will find a wealth of resources and crafters who can help troubleshoot and guide you in the right direction along the way if you need help or advice.

## DOUBLE CHECK YOUR COUNTERS

I suggest knitting a test sample, and counting along another way (either with pen and paper, or by using a hand counter) to test your machine counter to make sure it's working properly. If your row counter isn't working correctly, it could affect your work as you're following patterns.

## GET CREATIVE!

Circular knitting machines can be used for so many things—not just hats! They are fantastic for hats and headbands—but keep the door open to other ideas. Bags, dolls, homewear, decor, blankets, and so many other items can be made using circular knitting machines.

# Seaming the Ends

When you cast on and off using scrap yarn, the stitches will remain "live" for you to seam using a crochet hook or darning needle. Here, you'll learn how to crochet the ends closed when you cast on and off with scrap yarn.

Before you begin seaming, gently stretch out the stitches. If the cast on and cast off stitches look loose (the stitch near the yarn tails), pull the yarn tails gently to tighten them up a bit.

Rotate the piece so that the yarn tails are on the left side of the work.

Look at the open end of the tube, and close it flat, as in the next photo, with the yarn tails all the way to the left side. Identify the top line of stitches in the main color. You'll know which line of stitches to work through because it will be the very top line of main color stitches, directly above 1 line of scrap yarn stitches.

You'll begin seaming with the stitch all the way to the right side of the piece. This stitch will be perpendicular to the stitches to it's left side.

I like to use a size 3.5mm crochet hook, but you can use a different size hook if preferred. Begin by going under the first loop on the right side.

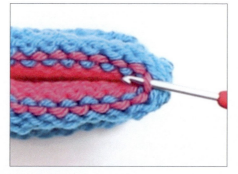

Then, pull through the loop **directly to it's left, on the top side**.

Next, pull through the stitch directly to it's left, on the bottom side.

Then, go back to the top row and pull through **the next loop directly to it's left.**

And back to the bottom row again. Pull through the **next loop directly to it's left on the bottom row.**

Continue in this pattern, alternating between pulling through one stitch on the top, followed by one stitch on the bottom, until the end of the row. Make sure to capture every single loop along the way.

When you reach the last stitch, wrap the yarn tail around the crochet hook.

Pull the yarn tail all the way through the loop to secure the tail with a knot.

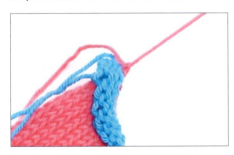

You'll now have a fully seamed side. The side will still have the scrap yarn attached.

The next step is to **remove the scrap yarn.** One side will usually pull off very easily—just pull the yarn and it will unwind and unwind until all of the stitches pull off. For the side that is more challenging to remove, identify the top length of yarn running through the top layer of stitches. Remove this length, a few stitches at a time, for the entire top row. Once that length is removed, the rest of the scrap yarn should pull off much more easily.

You'll now have one seamed side of your piece.

Turn the work around, and repeat the exact same process on the other side of the work to seam the other end of the piece. Remove the scrap yarn. You are done seaming the piece!

# Casting On and Off with Main Color

This is one of the the two main methods of casting on and off of a circular knitting machine. It's most commonly used when knitting hats, dolls, or any project where you want to "cinch" one or both sides of the work.

When knitting hats, dolls, or any projects where you'll be "cinching" one or both ends of the work, you'll likely want to cast on and off using the main color yarn. (**Without using scrap yarn**).

### FIND THE FIRST NEEDLE
Locate the first contrasting needle on your machine. On the Addi®, it will be the first black needle. On the Sentro™, it will be the only contrasting needle.

### CAST ON ROW
Using your main color yarn (the yarn you'll be knitting the piece with), wrap the yarn around the first needle with the yarn tail in the center. Leave a long tail in the yarn.

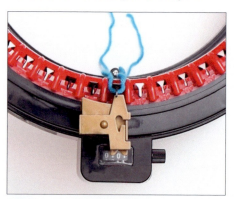

Then, using the working yarn (not the yarn tail), rotate the knob slowly and wrap the yarn around the **back of the second needle** and then in **front of the third needle.**

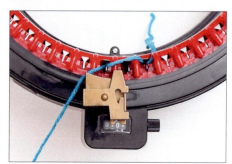

Continue in this process, wrapping the yarn back and forth along all the needles, until you reach the first needle again. Before you reach the needle where you first wrapped your scrap yarn, wrap the yarn behind the needle to it's right, and place the yarn into the yarn holder.

### KNITTING THE PIECE
If you're working with an Addi®, close the yarn holder. If you're working with a Sentro™, place it into the yarn holder and then place the yarn into the tensioner. If you're using an Addi, **hold the yarn in your left hand as you work to provide tension.**

You just finished your cast on row. Turn the knob and after a few stitches, set the counter back to zero. Continue knitting until you reach the first needle again.

When you reach the first needle again, you've just completed your first row of knitting. Continue knitting until your desired row count.

In this example, I've knit 20 rows, and now I'll be casting off with the main color yarn.

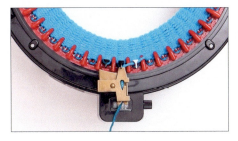

## CASTING OFF

Cut a long length in the yarn, at least enough to go around the width of your knitting machine a few times. Thread it onto a darning needle.

Turn the knob to advance a few needles. Identify the needle from where your yarn is emerging.

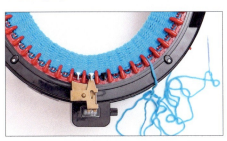

Throw the long yarn tail into the middle of the machine. **Begin by picking up the stitch directly to the left of the needle where your yarn is emerging from.** Work from the inside of the machine to the outside of the machine when picking up the stitches, and then pull the yarn through the stitch fully.

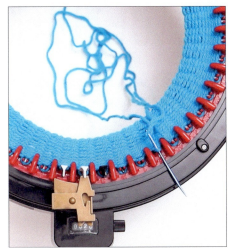

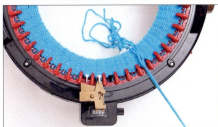

Continue picking up the stitches—one stitch at a time—for the first few stitches. After a few stitches, you can try picking up two stitches at a time. And about a third or halfway through the row, you can try picking up three stitches at a time. If you do pick them up more than one at a time, be sure not to pull any of the other stitches off the machine as you're working.

As you continue picking up the stitches, the work will begin to move from the machine to your yarn tail. Continue picking up all the stitches until the last stitch is on the yarn tail.

Your piece is now cast off and ready to assemble!

# Grafting Ends Together

Grafting the ends of knitting machine tubes together can be challenging at first—but once you get the hang of it, you can elevate many knitting machine projects by creating a seamless join of the ends.

Grafting the ends of knitting machine tubes together can seem intimidating at first. But after some practice, it will become easier, and it's a useful skill because it creates a seamless join between the ends. It's a great seam to use when knitting projects such as headbands, purses, or infinity scarves.

### STEP 1: CASTING ON AND OFF
When you graft knitting machine tube ends, **cast on and off using scrap yarn.** This will keep the stitches "live" and secure for when you're ready to graft. Always knit at least 5 rows in the scrap yarn. When you cast off, you always want to leave a long yarn tail in the main color yarn, which you'll use when grafting.

### STEP 2: LINING UP THE STITCHES
Bring the open ends of the tube together so that the open ends are facing either other. Line up the cast on and cast off stitches in the same place. (You'll know these stitches because they will have the yarn tails).

### STEP 3: GRAFTING
Bring the top layers together, as in the image above. Thread the bottom yarn tail onto a darning needle.

Thread the needle through the stitch directly above the yarn tail. Thread the needle **down through the first stitch,** and then **up through the stitch to it's left.** Pull the yarn through. Don't pull too tightly—keep the tension roughly similar to the knit stitches of the main piece.

Next, thread the needle through the stitch directly below the stitch you previously worked through. Again, thread the needle **down through the first stitch,** and **up through the stitch directly to it's left.** Pull the yarn through.

Next, go back to the top section. **Work the next stitch through the same stitch that you previously exited from on the last stitch of that row.** Repeat the same action: threading down through the first stitch, and up through the stitch to it's left. Pull the yarn through.

Again, go back to the bottom section, and **work the next stitch through the same stitch that you previously exited from on your last stitch of that row.** Pull the yarn through. Continue in this pattern, alternating between top and bottom stitches, until the end of the piece.

As you get to the edge of the outside, you'll need to turn the work inside out to finish seaming the inside of the work.

As you'll see in the photo above, as you work, you'll begin to create a new layer of stitches between the two ends of the work. Because of this, it's important not to pull the yarn too tightly as you work. If you pull too tightly, the stitches will look too small in comparison to the regular stitches. If you don't pull tightly enough, they will look too large. So keep an eye on the tension, and work to match the tension in the knit stitches above and below the grafted row.

Continue until the end of the row, making sure to capture all the last remaining stitches. After you do, secure the yarn tails with a few good knots. Remove the scrap yarn by unwinding around and around the work until the yarn falls off completely.

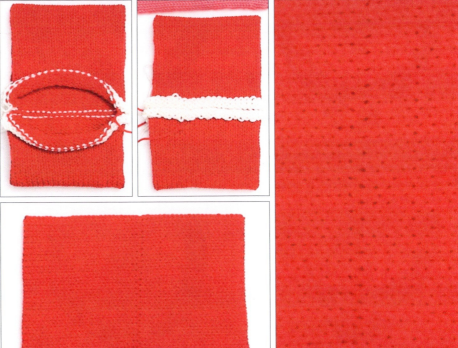

# Switching Colors

Switching colors on a circular knitting machine is easy—and it will unlock so many fun patterns—from striped hats, to checkered purses, and everything in between!

In this example, we'll be switching from red yarn to white yarn. In the photo below, I've finished my desired number of red rows, and the piece is ready to switch to white yarn.

Cut the yarn of the color you've just finished. Leave a 5 or 6" yarn tail.

Move the yarn to the inside of the machine after the needle at which you'd like to make the yarn change (typically at, or close, to the cast on needle)

Then, place the new color yarn in the same position that you previously had your previous yarn color. Place the yarn tails from the two yarn colors together, **between the same two needles**, and hold the two yarn tails together, close and low, as you slowly begin to knit the next row.

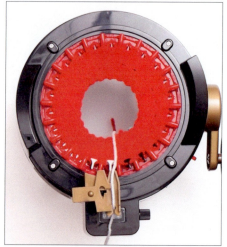

After you knit a few stitches, turn your counter back to zero to begin counting the rows in your next color.

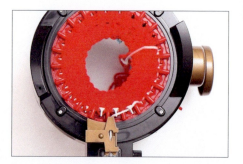

Continue knitting for about 5 rows. After you reach 5 rows of the new color, pause knitting and tie one quick, temporary knot between the two yarn tails.

**Note:** Only tie knots between yarn tails from interior work yarn color changes, **not between the scrap yarn tails and the cast on or cast off yarns.**

Now that your yarn color change tails have been secured with a quick knot (which will be finalized later, after you finish knitting the piece), you can continue knitting in the second color for as long as you need to reach your desired row count in that color. Make sure to remember to finalize the knots after the piece is finished knitting.

# Securing Yarn Color Change Tails

When you switch colors on a circular knitting machine, you'll end up with yarn tails on the inside of the work. You've tied a temporary knot while knitting, but you'll need to finalize and secure these knots after the knitting is done.

On the previous page, we looked at how to change colors when using a circular knitting machine. You'll notice that after 5 rows, you tied one quick, temporary knot between the yarn tails. After you've finished knitting the work, you'll need to come back to the piece to finalize and secure those knots.

You'll see in the image below that when you knit a piece with multiple yarn colors, each yarn change will leave 2 tails. Secure knots between all of the yarn tails **except for the yarn tails between the scrap yarn and the first color, and the scrap yarn and the last color**. Those tails should remain un-knotted.

For the yarn color change tails, secure each set of tails with a few good knots. As you're knotting the tails, look at the outside of the piece as you're working, to see how your tension is looking. You want to pull them tightly in order to bring the stitches together cleanly on the outside. However, you don't want to tie them *so* tightly that it bunches up your work. Especially for beginners, it's important to check back and forth as you're working

to see how the tension is looking on the outside.

After you've finished the knots, you can trim the tails down to a few inches. Because we're working with circular knit pieces in this pattern book, for most of the patterns here, you can leave the yarn tails in the center of the work. When working with circular knitting pieces, you don't need to weave in the yarn color changes like you would in a flat, hand-knit item. Simply secure with a knot, trim the tail, and turn the work right side out.

# Seaming with The Mattress Stitch

The Mattress Stitch is one of the most useful skills to have when working with circular knitting machine pieces. This stitch creates a seamless join and is the "glue" for many of the projects seen in this book.

The Mattress Stitch is used to join together two or more pieces of knitting. It creates a seamless join, either when working vertically or horizontally. This technique is used when creating projects like purses, fingerless gloves, and blankets.

### SEAMING VERTICAL PIECES
When seaming two pieces vertically, bring the two pieces together.

Identify the two lines of V-shaped stitches that you'll be joining. Make sure that the lines are running in the same direction (both sides are shaped like a "V").

Next, look for the interior bars that sit directly next to those two rows. (The bars to the right of the left side, and the bars to the left of the right side).

Before you begin, it can be helpful to join the two sides together temporarily using stitch markers. When you place the stitch markers, place them in the first half of the V-shaped stitch **below the interior bars** you plan to use for the join.

When you work the Mattress Stitch, thread a length of yarn (often the yarn tail from the project) onto a darning needle and thread through one of the interior bars we located earlier. Pull the yarn through.

Next, thread the darning needle through the corresponding interior bar on the other side of the work. And pull the yarn through. Remove the stitch markers as you approach them.

Continue alternating back and forth between one interior bar on one side, and one interior bar on the other side, until the end of the row. When you're connecting two pieces **vertically**, it's important to pull the yarn somewhat tightly as you work. This will help create a clean seam. When you reach the end of the work, secure the yarn with a few good knots and weave in the ends.

As you work, you'll see that the Mattress Stitch creates a seamless join.

## WORKING TWO BARS AT A TIME
If you're seaming a large piece (such as a blanket), you can work the Mattress Stitch two bars at a time, instead of one bar at a time. This will speed up the process significantly, and will still create a strong and seamless join.

## SEAMING HORIZONTAL PIECES
If you're seaming two horizontal pieces of knitting together, thread your yarn (or yarn tail) onto a darning needle and thread through both halves of one of the V-shaped stitches on the edge of one side, and pull the yarn through.

Then, thread through both halves of one of the V-shaped stitches on the other edge. Pull the yarn through. As you're working this stitch, **do not pull the yarn tightly**, as you do when seaming vertical pieces together. You will essentially be creating a new row of stitches, so you'll want the stitches to be approximately the same tension as the knit stitches above and below that row.

## SEAMING A HORIZONTAL SIDE WITH A VERTICAL SIDE
If you're seaming the horizontal edge of one piece to the vertical edge of another, you'll use a mix of these two techniques. For the side where you're picking up stitches on the vertical side, thread through one interior bar to the side of the V-shaped stitches.

Then, thread through both halves of the corresponding V-shaped stitch on the horizontal side of the other piece.

As you work, you may need to occasionally work through two interior bars on the vertical side in order to "catch up" with the side with the V-shaped stitches.

**Note:** One of the most important parts of creating a nice looking seam is to be consistent and follow along the exact same row of stitches from beginning to end. If you accidentally "switch" rows partway through, the seam will not look right at that area. Using stitch markers in advance can help a lot with this, especially for long pieces of knitting.

# Knitting Long Pieces

There are two ways to manage the work when knitting long pieces: you can roll the work up inside the machine, or you can set up your machine so that the work can fall down lower than the table.

When knitting longer pieces, such as a scarf, or blanket pieces, there are a few ways to manage the work as you are knitting. You can roll the work up as you work, or you can set up your machine so that there is space under the machine for the work to fall into.

### OPTION 1: ROLLING THE WORK

If you have your machine attached to a regular table, you'll need to roll the work up inside the machine as you knit. In the photo below, the piece I'm knitting has just started to touch the table at the bottom.

This is the point at which you should bring the work up inside the machine. At first, you can simply fold it up inside the machine. However, as you continue knitting, and the work gets longer, you'll need to roll the work as you're knitting.

### OPTION 2: CREATE SPACE UNDER

This can be achieved a few ways. Some knitters will design a desk that has a hole custom-built for working with circular knitting machines. If you don't have a custom table available, you can achieve similar functionality by clamping your machine legs to two different tables. The tables should be the exact same height as each other. By placing the center of the machine over the space between the tables, it will give some additional room for the work to fall while you're knitting.

# Sewing in Zippers

Sewing a zipper into a knitted item is a helpful skill to have, especially when knitting purses and bags, including the phone wristlet shown in this book.

The first step when sewing a zipper into a knitted item is to make sure you have enough room for your zipper. For instance, if you want to sew in a zipper that is 8" long, you'll want to make sure that the knitted piece is approximately 8.5-9" long.

For this example, I'll be showing how to sew an 8" zipper into a bag.

First, if you plan to add a knitting tag to the top of the bag, add it before you begin sewing.

Place one side of the zipper into the top of the bag, and secure it with pins. Place it so that the zipper part is aligned with the top of the bag (not above it).

Use a thread that is similar in color to the main color yarn. Thread into a sewing needle and pull the thread through so that it's doubled. Tie a few knots at the bottom of the thread. Begin threading from **the inside-back of the fabric** so that the knot is hidden in the back of the fabric.

Thread the needle through the fabric to the exterior of the piece. When you work the exterior stitches, **thread the needle over the interior bars, and not over the V-shaped stitches.** This will help create a cleaner seam.

As you work, you can use a regular sewing stitch, or you can sew using a back stitch. If you placed a knitting tag at the top, sew as closely as possible to the knitting tag, and then sew only in the fabric behind the tag, and again picking up the sewing as closely as possible immediately after the tag.

Continue sewing until the end of the zipper. When you reach the corner, unzip and fold over the zipper, and place it into the other side of the bag using pins. Continue sewing in the same way until the end of the row.

For a stronger seam, repeat the same process again on the bottom of the fabric, for two sewing rows.

When you're done, secure the thread with a few good knots on the inside of the fabric. If you end up with extra space on the sides of the zipper, you can use the main color yarn to stitch over the open space if need be. Your zipper is done!

# Using an I-Cord Machine

I-Cord machines are a fun and quick way to knit I-Cords. These cords can be used for purse handles, jewelry, home decor projects, bows, word art and more.

For this demonstration, I'm using the Tulip™ I-Cord knitter machine. However, there are numerous I-Cord knitting machines on the market. The machine comes with two pieces: the knitting machine, and a weight.

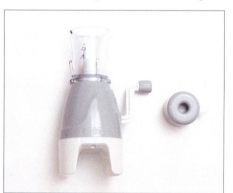

The first step is to thread your yarn through the loop on the left side, over the top (resting in the groove), and down through the middle of the machine, until the yarn is coming out of the bottom.

For photographic purposes, my machine is lying down on table. But when knitting, you'll be hold the machine upright, with the yarn held tightly in your left hand to provide tension.

Add the weight to the bottom of the yarn, so that when you hold the machine in the air, it's pulling down on the yarn as you knit.

## CASTING ON
Make sure that all 4 hooks are open. Turn the knob slowly, and **allow the first hook capture the yarn.**

Turn the knob again, but stop before the second hook captures the yarn. Use your fingers or a crochet hook to **move the yarn behind the second hook.**

Turn the knob again, and **allow the third needle to capture the yarn.**

Turn the knob again, and like earlier, stop before the fourth hook captures the yarn. Use your fingers or a crochet hook to **move the yarn behind the fourth hook.**

## KNITTING THE I-CORD

Your cast on row is now complete. To knit the I-Cord, simply turn the knob until your work reaches the desired length. Unlike the cast on row, you will allow all 4 stitches to capture the stitches on every row.

As you work, make sure to keep an eye on two things: 1) Make sure to continue **holding the yarn firmly in your left hand to provide tension**, and 2) Make sure **the weight is continuing to pull down on the yarn** as you are knitting.

Soon, you will see the I-Cord begin to emerge from the bottom of the machine.

Continue knitting until your I-Cord is the desired length—or longer—for your project. Always err on the side of longer, rather than shorter, when knitting I-Cords with your machine, because it's very easy to pull the stitches out to shorten the length. But, it would be a lot of work to add length to the I-Cord after it's off the machine.

## CASTING OFF

When your I-Cord is your desired length, cut a tail in the yarn (at least 6-10" if you'll be using the yarn tail to attach the I-Cord (as a handle, for example). Unhook a stitch or two and then continue knitting until the work pops off the needles. Now, you can simply pull the I-Cord out from the bottom of the machine.

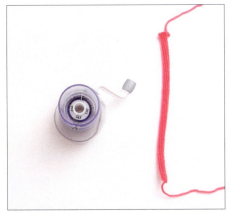

## BINDING OFF

The bottom of the I-Cord will already be secured with a knot. However, you'll notice that the top of the I-Cord will have 4 live stitches. At this point, if you'd like to shorten the length of your I-Cord, simply pinch at the area of your desired length, and pull the yarn tail to pull out the stitches until you reach your fingers.

Thread the yarn tail onto a darning needle. Gently thread the yarn through all four live stitches. Be careful while you work so that you don't accidentally pull out any of the stitches. After you've captured all four stitches, secure the yarn tail with a couple of good knots to secure the end.

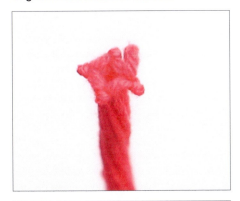

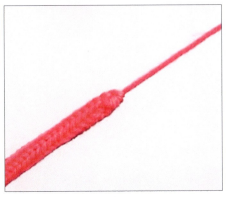

Your I-Cord is complete!

# Assembling a Hat

Hats are one of the most frequently made projects with a circular knitting machine! There are a few ways to assemble the hats—here's one method.

To knit a hat, follow the instructions on pages 16-17 to cast on and off using the main color yarn. (**Do not use scrap yarn**). Row counts vary depending on the size hat you're knitting; however, a common row count for adult sized hats is 110 rows (without a brim) or 140 rows (with a brim). Both the 46 needle Addi® Express Kingsize and the 48 needle Sentro™ are commonly used for hats. The 46 needle Addi® Express Kingsize will make a slightly smaller hat, and the 48 needle Sentro will make a slightly larger hat (a 2 stitch difference in width). You can adjust the sizing slightly with your tension. With tighter tension, the hat will be smaller—with looser tension, the hat will be larger.

When you finish your desired row count, use a darning needle to pick up all the stitches off the machine.

When you pull the work out of the machine, the stitches will be bunched up tightly as in the following photo.

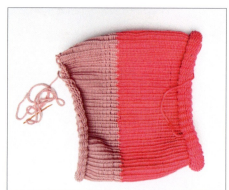

Gently pull the work to stretch out the stitches.

If you switched colors in your hat, turn the work inside out before proceeding, and secure the yarn tails with a few good knots. You can leave the ends loose, as they will end up in the center of the hat. If you're knitting a hat with only one color, skip this step.

Turn the work right side out. Use one of the yarn tails to cinch one end of the work. As you cinch, the work may start rolling outward—if this happens, use your fingers to roll the work inside.

One side will now be cinched, and one side will still be open.

Thread the yarn tail onto a darning needle and secure the cinched side with a few knots. Then, thread the darning needle into the center.

Bring the cinched side inside the work to the open end of the work, and pull the darning needle to bring the yarn tail to the top of the hat.

Next, cinch the top layer of the hat in the same process as earlier. Use the yarn tail to cinch the work, making sure to roll the work inside as you cinch.

When you finish cinching the top, you'll see two yarn tails—one from each side, emerging from the top of the hat. Tie a few good knots between the two yarn tails. Tie as tightly as you can without breaking the yarn.

Next, thread the yarn tails onto a darning needle and hide the yarn tails in the center of the work, between the inner and outer layers of the hat, and trim the tails.

If desired, add a knitting tag and/or pom pom. This technique is also used for making stuffed animals. If you're making a stuffed animal, fill the inside with stuffing, and then thread a length of yarn onto a darning needle and pick up the first half of each stitch on the bottom of the work, and cinch the bottom closed.

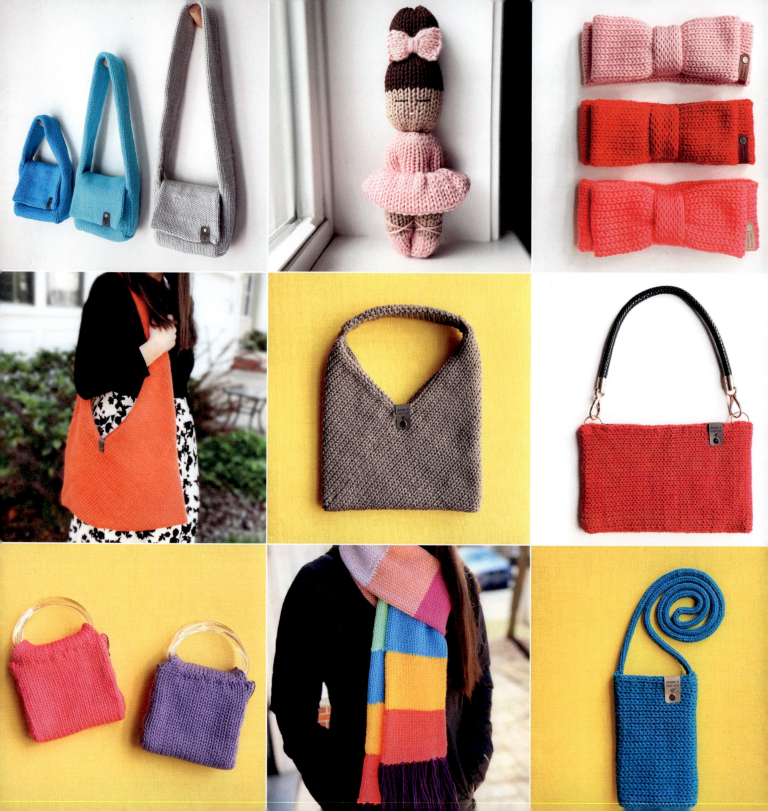

# The Patterns

# Messenger Bag Purses

SIZING:
Approximately
8" wide x 8" tall
(without the handle)

These bags are cozy, functional, and you can easily customize the size by knitting a longer or shorter handle. They are the perfect size to fit a phone, wallet, keys and a few other small items.

## Supplies

- ☐ 46 or 48 needle circular knitting machine
- ☐ 22 needle circular knitting machine
- ☐ Weight 4/Medium yarn
- ☐ Crochet hook
- ☐ Darning needle
- ☐ Scissors
- ☐ An item 2-3" tall for support when seaming
- ☐ Stitch markers
- ☐ Knitting tag (optional)

## Quick Recipe

**MAIN PIECE:**
- 46 or 48 needle machine
- Cast on and off with scrap yarn
- Knit 110 rows

**HANDLE (SMALL):**
- 22 needle machine
- Cast on and off with scrap yarn
- Knit 130 rows

**HANDLE (MEDIUM):**
- 22 needle machine
- Cast on and off with scrap yarn
- Knit 200 rows

**HANDLE (LARGE):**
- 22 needle machine
- Cast on and off with scrap yarn
- Knit 250 rows

### STEP 1: KNITTING THE MAIN PIECE
Cast on to a 46 or 48 needle circular knitting machine using scrap yarn. **Knit 5 rows in the scrap yarn.** Switch to the main color. **Knit 110 rows in the main color.** (If you'd like a taller bag, knit more rows. If you'd like a shorter bag, knit less rows). Switch back to scrap yarn. **Knit 5 rows in the scrap yarn.** Cut the yarn and continue knitting until the work falls off the needles. Remove the work from the machine and gently stretch out the stitches. Put aside the work for now, while you knit the handle.

### STEP 2: KNITTING THE HANDLE
Cast on to a 22 needle circular knitting machine. **Knit 5 rows in the scrap yarn.** Switch to the main color. **For the small size: Knit 130 rows in the main color. For the medium size: Knit 200 rows in the main color. For the large size: Knit 250 rows in the main color.** Switch back to scrap yarn. **Knit 5 rows in the scrap yarn.** Remove the work from the machine and gently stretch out the stitches.

### STEP 3: SEAMING THE ENDS
Use a crochet hook to seam the open ends of the tubes closed. (See pages 14-15 for details).

### STEP 4: ASSEMBLE THE BAG
Lay your main piece vertically. Fold the bottom third up. Then, fold the top third down. Line up the handles on the sides, as shown in the diagram. Find an item about 2-3" high (such as a roll of packing tape) and place it in the center of the bag, to provide support. The bottom third should measure

approximately 6" tall. Join the sides of the bag with stitch markers, including markers at all 4 bottom corners.

### STEP 5: THE MATTRESS STITCH
Cut a length of yarn twice as long as the area you'll be seaming. Use the Mattress Stitch (see pages 22-23 for details) to seam the bag, starting with the front top left corner, following along the bag until the top back left corner. **Make sure to end the back at the same height as the front.** Repeat the same process on the other side of the bag.

### STEP 6: FINAL TOUCHES
Weave in and trim all the ends. If desired, add a knitting tag. If you'd like to add some extra support, cut a piece of cardboard a little smaller than the bottom and place it into the bottom of the bag. For more support, line the inside of the bag with fabric.

# Geometric Handbags

**SIZING:** Approximately 9" wide x 13" tall (with the handle)

Use the leftover yarn in your yarn stash to make this multicolor, geometric bag! Or, knit it up all in one color for a simple, sophisticated look. Find a blank template on pages 112-113 to sketch out your design in advance.

## Supplies

- [ ] 22 needle circular knitting machine
- [ ] I-Cord knitting machine
- [ ] Weight 4/Medium yarn
- [ ] Crochet hook
- [ ] Darning needle
- [ ] Scissors
- [ ] Knitting tag (optional)

## Quick Recipe

- 22 needle machine
- Cast on and off with scrap yarn

**PIECE 1:**
- Square 1: Knit 16 rows
- Square 2: Knit 16 rows

**PIECE 2:**
- Square 1: Knit 16 rows
- Square 2: Knit 15 rows
- Square 3: Knit 16 rows

**PIECE 3:**
- Square 1: Knit 16 rows
- Square 2: Knit 15 rows
- Square 3: Knit 15 rows
- Square 4: Knit 16 rows

**PIECE 4:**
- Square 1: Knit 16 rows
- Square 2: Knit 15 rows
- Square 3: Knit 16 rows

**PIECE 5**
- Square 1: Knit 17 rows

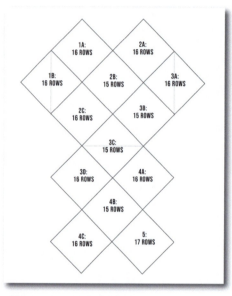

1A: 16 ROWS | 2A: 16 ROWS
1B: 16 ROWS | 2B: 15 ROWS | 3A: 16 ROWS
2C: 16 ROWS | 3B: 15 ROWS
3C: 15 ROWS
3D: 16 ROWS | 4A: 16 ROWS
4B: 15 ROWS
4C: 16 ROWS | 5: 17 ROWS

### STEP 1: FOLLOWING THE CHART

This bag is knit in 5 pieces. Follow the graph above, knitting pieces 1, 2, 3, 4, and 5 beginning with the top square, and continuing until the bottom square. For example, for piece 2, you'll knit 2A (16 rows), 2B (15 rows), and then 2C (16 rows).

As you work, cast on and off before the **first needle**, but when you change your yarn colors in the interior of the pieces, knit 3 additional stitches after you reach your desired row count, and switch after the **third needle**. This will "move" your yarn changes to the inside of the bag, which will create a cleaner seam. As you work, leave a 2' yarn tail when you cast on and off, in both your first and last square colors, which you'll use later when seaming the bag.

### STEP 2: KNITTING THE PIECES

**Piece 1:** Cast on to a 22 needle machine with scrap yarn. **Knit 5 rows in the scrap yarn.** Switch to 1A's color, leaving a 2' yarn tail. **Knit 16 rows in 1A's color.** Switch to 1B's color, leaving a 5" tail in both colors (as for all the following interior yarn color changes). **Knit 16 rows.** After a few rows, tie a quick temporary knot between the two yarn tails (as for all the following interior yarn color changes). You'll secure them better later, so just one temporary knot is great. After you finish 1B, switch back to the scrap yarn, again leaving a 2' tail in the 1B color, and **knit 5 rows in the scrap yarn.** Then, cut the scrap yarn and continue knitting until the work falls off the needles. Gently stretch out the stitches and set the piece aside for now while you knit the remaining 4 pieces.

**Piece 2:** Cast on to a 22 needle machine with scrap yarn. **Knit 5 rows in the scrap yarn. Knit 16 rows in 2A's color. Knit 15 rows in 2B's color. Knit 16 rows in 2C's color. Knit 5 rows in the scrap yarn,** and cast the work off the machine.

**Piece 3:** Cast on to a 22 needle machine with scrap yarn. **Knit 5 rows in the scrap**

yarn. **Knit 16 rows in 3A's color. Knit 15 rows in 3B's color. Knit 15 rows in 3C's color. Knit 16 rows in 3D's color. Knit 5 rows in the scrap yarn** and cast the work off the machine.

**Piece 4:** Cast on to a 22 needle machine with scrap yarn. **Knit 5 rows in the scrap yarn. Knit 16 rows in 4A's color. Knit 15 rows in 4B's color. Knit 16 rows in 4C's color. Knit 5 rows in the scrap yarn** and cast the work off the machine.

**Piece 5:** Cast on to a 22 needle machine with scrap yarn. **Knit 5 rows in the scrap yarn. Knit 17 rows in 5's color. Knit 5 rows in the scrap yarn** and cast the work off the machine.

### STEP 3: SEAMING THE ENDS
You'll now have 5 knit pieces with open ends. Turn the first four tubes inside out, and secure the yarn change tails with a few good knots (except for the tails between the cast on and cast off switches), checking the outside as you work to make sure you're pulling the knots tight, but not too tight.

Turn the pieces right side out and use a crochet hook to seam the open ends of the tubes closed. (See pages 14-15 for details). Remove the scrap yarn.

### STEP 4: ASSEMBLING THE BAG
Place your tubes as directed in the graph on the previous page. If helpful, attach the sides using stitch markers to pull the work together as you seam. Using the long yarn tails and a darning needle, use the Mattress Stitch (see details on pages 22-23) to seam the sides of the tubes together, working 2 stitches at a time. After you finish each row,

secure the yarn tails with a few good knots on the back of the work (which will later be the inside of the bag).

Turn the work over (with the back of the piece facing up), and bring the bottom to the the top. Then, fold the left and right sides in.

Next, seam the sides of the bag, beginning from the bottom, and working your way to the top. For these seams, make sure to use a length of yarn or yarn tail in the same color as one of the squares you're seaming, because the yarn will be visible on some parts of the sides. For these seams, work 1 stitch at a time, unless the work isn't matching up evenly, in which case you

can occasionally thread through 2 stitches on one side to even out the seam. When you seam the sides that are horizontal (as opposed to the vertical sides we often use for the Mattress Stitch), work through the V-shaped stitches as shown above. When you work these seams, don't pull too tight.

When you finish seaming the bag, you'll have many yarn tails left over. Turn the bag inside out, make sure all the yarn tails are secure with knots, and thread them onto darning needles to weave them into the center of the work.

### STEP 5: KNITTING THE HANDLES
Use an I-Cord machine, or hand-knit two I-Cords in the desired length for your handles. (See pages 26-27 for details). Attach them securely to the corners of the bag, working through numerous times to ensure a secure join. Tie a knot with the yarn tail on an interior bar, and weave the tail up through the handle and trim. If desired, add a knitting tag to the center of the bag, or your preferred location. Your bag is complete!

# Striped Handbag

**SIZING:**
Approximately
9" wide x 13" tall
(with the handle)

A simpler take on the Geometric handbag, choose two contrasting colors to create a striking look. Or, use the same color for all the pieces for a simpler look. Find a blank template on page 114-115, to design your bag!

## Supplies

- [ ] 22 needle circular knitting machine
- [ ] I-Cord knitting machine
- [ ] Weight 4/Medium yarn
- [ ] Crochet hook
- [ ] Darning needle
- [ ] Scissors
- [ ] Knitting tag (optional)

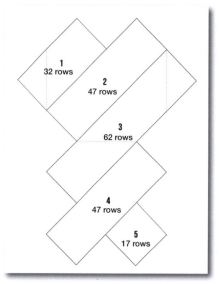

### Quick Recipe

- 22 needle knitting machine
- Cast on and off with scrap yarn

**PIECE 1:** Knit 32 rows
**PIECE 2:** Knit 47 rows
**PIECE 3:** Knit 62 rows
**PIECE 4:** Knit 47 rows
**PIECE 5:** Knit 17 rows

### STEP 1: FOLLOWING THE CHART
To knit this bag, follow all the same steps as the Geometric bag (pages 34-37). However, in this bag, you'll be following the chart displayed to the right.

### STEP 2: KNITTING THE PIECES
**Piece 1:** Cast on to a 22 needle circular knitting machine using scrap yarn. **Knit 5 rows in the scrap yarn.** Switch to the color for your first piece, leaving a 2' yarn tail (as for all the following cast on tails). **Knit 32 rows in the main color.** Switch back to scrap yarn, leaving another 2' yarn tail in the main color (as for all following cast off tails). **Knit 5 rows in the scrap yarn.** Cut the scrap yarn, and continue knitting until the work falls off the needles. Gently stretch out the stitches and put the work aside while you knit the next four pieces.

**Piece 2:** Cast on to a 22 needle circular knitting machine using scrap yarn. **Knit 5 rows in the scrap yarn.** Switch to the color for Piece 2, leaving a long tail. **Knit 47 rows in the main color.** Switch back to the scrap yarn. **Knit 5 rows in the scrap yarn.** Cut the yarn and cast off the stitches.

**Piece 3:** Cast on to a 22 needle circular knitting machine using scrap yarn. **Knit 5 rows in the scrap yarn.** Switch to the color for Piece 3, leaving a long tail. **Knit 62 rows in the main color.** Switch back to the scrap yarn. **Knit 5 rows in the scrap yarn.** Cut the yarn and cast off the stitches.

**Piece 4:** Cast on to a 22 needle circular knitting machine using scrap yarn. **Knit 5 rows in the scrap yarn.** Switch to the color for Piece 4, leaving a long tail. **Knit 47 rows in the main color.** Switch back to the scrap yarn. **Knit 5 rows in the scrap yarn.** Cut the yarn and cast off the stitches.

**Piece 5:** Cast on to a 22 needle circular knitting machine using scrap yarn. **Knit 5 rows in the scrap yarn.** Switch to the color for Piece 5, leaving a long tail. **Knit 17 rows in the main color.** Switch back to the scrap yarn. **Knit 5 rows in the scrap yarn.** Cut the yarn and cast off the stitches.

### STEP 3: SEAMING THE ENDS
Use a crochet hook to seam the open ends of the tubes closed. (See pages 14-15 for details). Remove the scrap yarn.

### STEP 4: ASSEMBLING THE BAG
To finish the bag, follow steps 4 and 5 of the "Geometric Bag" pattern on page 37.

# Ballerina Doll

SIZING:
Approximately
3" wide x 10" tall

This doll is so easy to customize—you can switch up the yarn colors, change the bow, play with different facial features—or knit the skirt in a few different colors, and make a "dress up doll"! Find a blank template on pages 116-117.

## Supplies

- [ ] 22 needle circular knitting machine
- [ ] 46 or 48 needle circular knitting machine
- [ ] Weight 4/Medium yarn
- [ ] Crochet hook
- [ ] Darning needle
- [ ] Scissors
- [ ] Hair elastic
- [ ] Embroidery thread or black yarn
- [ ] Size US 7 (4.5mm) knitting needles
- [ ] Knitting tag (optional)

## Quick Recipe

**DOLL:**
- 22 needle knitting machine
- Cast on and off with **main colors**

1) 22 rows: Hair
2) 11 rows: Face
3) 14 rows: Shirt
4) 12 rows: Legs
5) 10 rows: Ballet slippers
6) 12 rows: Legs
7) 14 rows: Shirt
8) 11 rows: Face
9) 22 rows: Hair

**SKIRT:**
- 46 or 48 needle machine
- Cast on and off with **scrap yarn**
- Knit 18 rows in skirt color

### STEP 1: KNITTING THE MAIN PIECE
Cast on to a 22 needle circular knitting machine, using the hair color yarn. **Knit 22 rows in the hair color.** Switch to the face yarn and **knit 11 rows.** Switch to the shirt yarn and **knit 14 rows.** Switch to the legs yarn and **knit 12 rows.** Switch to the ballet slippers yarn and **knit 10 rows.**

Switch back to the legs yarn and **knit 12 rows.** Switch back to the shirt yarn and **knit 14 rows.** Switch back to the face yarn and **knit 11 rows.** Switch back to the hair yarn and **knit 22 rows.**

Cut a long tail in the hair yarn and thread it onto a darning needle. Pick up all the stitches on the machine using the darning needle. (See details on pages 16-17)

### STEP 2: KNITTING THE SKIRT
Cast on to a 46 or 48 needle circular knitting machine with a scrap yarn. **Knit 5 rows in the scrap yarn.** Switch to the skirt color. **Knit 18 rows in the skirt color.** Switch back to the scrap yarn. **Knit 5 rows in the scrap yarn.** Cut the yarn and continue knitting until the work falls off the needles. Pull the work out of the machine and gently stretch out the stitches.

### STEP 3: ASSEMBLING THE DOLL
Stretch out the work and turn it inside out. Finalize all of the yarn tails with a few good knots, and trim the tails to a couple of inches. Turn the work right side out.

Cinch one end of the tube using the yarn tail. Then, push that side up within the tube to meet the other hair side. Thread the cinched side's yarn tail onto a darning needle and push it out to the top of the head. Tie the two yarn tails from both sides together tightly, and then weave in the ends to the center of the work. Look for the side that has the yarn changes, and use that side as the back of the doll.

### STEP 4: ADD STUFFING
Slowly add stuffing to the inside of the doll. Don't overstuff. Gently push the stuffing to the areas where it's needed. When you're done, thread a length of yarn in the ballet shoes color and secure it with a knot on an interior bar stitch on the back of the doll. Thread the needle through the first half of each V-shaped stitch around the bottom of the feet, and then cinch the bottom closed and secure with a knot, and weave in the ends.

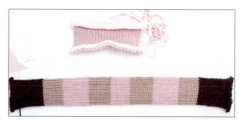

### STEP 5: SHAPING THE BODY & FACE

Create the neck by threading a length of the face yarn onto a darning needle, securing with a knot on the back, on an interior bar stitch, and then threading the yarn through the first half of each V-shaped stitch around the neck until you reach the back again. Pull the yarn tight to create the neck. Secure with a knot and then wrap the yarn around the outside one time, pull tightly and secure with another knot in the back. Repeat the same process about 1/3 way down from the top of her head, to create the bun.

Next, create the legs. Using shoe color yarn, secure with a knot on an interior bar stitch on the back of the doll, and then sew up from the feet until you reach the legs. Then, thread the yarn back to the back, secure with a knot and weave in the ends. Then repeat the same process with the leg color yarn, and sew back and forth until 1cm before the shirt.

Next, add the ballet slipper straps. Use the ballet shoe yarn and secure with a knot on the back of the doll. Wrap the yarn to create an X, threading the yarn through one interior side stitch (further to the back) to keep the yarn in place on the side.

Next, create the arms. Use a length of shirt color yarn to sew up in a line, about 1.5cm from the side, stopping about 2cm from the neck.

Then, use embroidery thread or yarn to create eyes and a mouth. Secure the thread with a knot on an interior bar on the back, thread it to the front, then to the back, and repeat for the other eye.

### STEP 6: SEAM THE SKIRT

Turn the skirt inside out, with the V-shaped stitches on the inside. Wrap a hair elastic around the center. Line up the top main color stitches and use a crochet hook to go under a loop on the bottom. Pull through the loop directly above it. Then, pull through the loop to the left of it on the top side (as if seaming a scrunchie). Then, pull through the loop to the left of it on the bottom side. Continue alternating between top and bottom loops until the end of the row. When you reach the end, tie a knot between the yarn tails. Next, remove the scrap yarn. If you'd like to add a knitting tag, add it to the skirt. **If giving this doll to a child, do not use any items that could be pulled off.** You can either attach the skirt permanently, or create a few different skirts that can be changed, like a "dress up doll."

### STEP 7: KNIT THE BOW

There are many ways to create a bow for the doll, including crochet or knitting. Here is a hand-knit pattern for the bow. Cast on 10 stitches to a US Size 7 knitting needle using The Long Tail Cast On Method. Knit 2.5" in Double Stockinette stitch: K1, SL1 WYIF* repeat until end of row (Knit 1 stitch, slip 1 stitch with yarn in front* repeat until end of row, for every row) When you reach 2.5", bind off in pattern. Cut a long length in the bow color yarn and wrap it around the middle of the bow. Secure the yarn tails with a few good knots on the back of the bow. If you want the bow to be taken on and off, tie it on the doll's hair bun just like you would tie shoes. If you want it to be secured onto the doll permanently, stitch it through and secure it with knots and weave in the ends. Your doll is complete!

This bag is very simple—knit one piece for the bag, and one piece for the handle. It makes a great gift, and can be customized in so many ways. If desired, use a longer handle to make it a shoulder bag!

# SUPPLIES

- [ ] 48 needle circular knitting machine
- [ ] Weight 4/Medium yarn
- [ ] Crochet hook
- [ ] Darning needle
- [ ] Scissors
- [ ] Knitting tag (optional)

## QUICK RECIPE

**MAIN PIECE:**
- 48 needle knitting machine
- Cast on and off with scrap yarn
- **Knit 110 rows**

**HANDLE:**
- 48 needle machine
- Cast on and off with scrap yarn
- **Knit 8 rows**

## STEP 1: KNITTING THE MAIN PIECE
Cast on to a 48 needle circular knitting machine using scrap yarn. **Knit 5 rows in the scrap yarn.** Switch to your main color yarn, leaving a yarn tail of at least a few feet, which you'll use to seam the bag later. **Knit 110 rows in the main color.** When you finish the main color, switch back to the scrap yarn. **Knit 5 rows in the scrap yarn.** Then, cut the scrap yarn and continue knitting until the work falls off the needles. Pull the work out of the machine and gently stretch out the stitches. Set the work aside for now while you knit the handle.

**Note:** For this pattern, it's important that your dimensions match the dimensions of the piece shown below. Tension can vary from person to person and yarn to yarn—so if your piece is too long or too short, adapt the row count so that it matches the dimensions shown below. You might need to knit a few rows more or less than 110 to match the dimensions.

## STEP 2: KNITTING THE HANDLE
There are numerous ways to knit the handle for this piece. You can crochet, hand knit, or braid the handle, or you could use an I-Cord. However for this project, we are using the same 48 needle circular knitting machine.

Cast on to a 48 needle circular knitting machine with scrap yarn. **Knit 5 rows in the scrap yarn.** Switch to the main color, leaving a long yarn tail. **Knit 8 rows in the main color.** Switch back to the scrap yarn, again leaving a long tail in the main color. **Knit 5 rows in the scrap yarn.** Cut the scrap yarn and continue knitting until the work falls off the needles. Pull the work out of the machine and gently stretch out the stitches.

## STEP 3: SEAMING THE ENDS
Use a crochet hook to seam the open ends of the tubes closed. (See page 14-15 for details). Remove the scrap yarn.

You'll now have two seamed pieces. The handle should measure approximately 7.5" x 1.5" and the main piece should measure approximately 22" long x 7.5" wide.

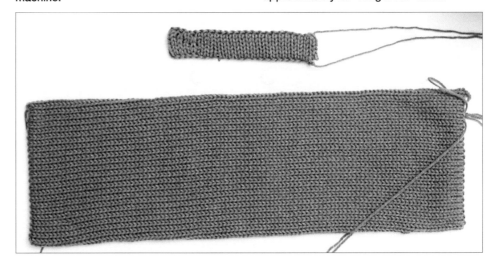

# TOTE BAGS ...CONTINUED

### STEP 4: ASSEMBLING THE BAG

To assemble the bag, fold the right corner down. Then, fold the left corner up. Then, fold Corner A up to create the shape in photo. The inner corners of A and B will meet as the center-top of the bag. Use stitch markers to secure the bag in shape before seaming.

### STEP 5: SEAMING THE BAG

Use the Mattress Stitch to seam both sides of the bag (see pages 22-23 for details). As you work, take care to make sure that you

are staying within the same row the entire way down. Pull the yarn tightly as you work, to make a secure seam.

### STEP 5: ATTACHING THE HANDLES

Use the yarn tail from the handle piece and a darning needle to sew the handles to the sides of the bag. The sides of the bag are corners, so sew half of the handle to one side of the corner, and half of the handle to the other side of the corner. For the first and last stitches, bring the yarn through both stitches like a normal sewing stitch. And for the middle stitches, switch back to the Mattress Stitch. When you finish, secure the yarn tails with knots and weave the ends into the center of the work.

Repeat the same process on the other side. When you're done, make sure you go back to the inside of the bag, secure any remaining yarn tails and weave in the ends into the center of the work with a darning needle.

When you finish seaming, you might notice a small gap in the middle center of the top of the bag. If this happens, use a length of yarn in the main color to stitch up the gap, and then secure with a knot and weave in the ends.

Lastly, if desired, add a knitting tag to the work. You can place it in the center of the bag as shown to the right, or you can place it anywhere else along the bag.

There are many ways to customize this bag. You can knit a longer handle to turn it into a shoulder bag. If you prefer a firmer bag, you can line the inside of the bag with fabric. You could add a magnetic clasp to the top-inside area, or you could add a button closure. Your bag is complete!

SIZING:
Approximately
19" wide x 22" tall
(with the handle)

# Large Tote Bags

These totes are large and roomy—and because they're knit, they also keep you cozy and warm! This pattern requires a lot of seaming, but it's worth the effort!

## Supplies

- [ ] 46 or 48 needle knitting machine
- [ ] 22 needle knitting machine
- [ ] Weight 4/Medium yarn
- [ ] Crochet hook
- [ ] Darning needle
- [ ] Scissors
- [ ] Stitch markers
- [ ] Knitting tag (optional)

## Quick Recipe

**MAIN PIECES (KNIT 2):**
- 46 or 48 needle machine
- Cast on and off with scrap yarn
- 46 needle machine: **Knit 218 rows**
- 48 needle machine: **Knit 220 rows**

**HANDLE:**
- 22 needle machine
- Cast on and off with scrap yarn
- **Knit 25 to 100 rows**

### STEP 1: KNITTING THE MAIN PIECE

Cast on to a 46 or 48 needle circular knitting machine, using scrap yarn. **Knit 5 rows in the scrap yarn.** Switch to the main color yarn, leaving a very, very long tail to use when seaming the bag together. **If you're using a 46 needle machine, knit 218 rows in the main color. If you're using a 48 needle machine, knit 220 rows in the main color.** Switch back to the scrap yarn, again leaving a very, very long tail in

the main color. **Knit 5 rows in the scrap yarn.** Then, cut the scrap yarn and continue knitting until the work falls off the needles. Pull the work out of the machine and gently stretch out the stitches. Put the work aside for now, while you knit the second piece.

Repeat the same process one more time to knit the second piece. It's important that the two pieces are the **exact same length**, so be careful to keep an eye on the counter and make sure both pieces have the exact same row count. If they are off by one or two rows, it should be okay. But if they are off by much more than that, the piece won't match up.

**Note:** For this pattern, it's important that your dimensions match the dimensions of the piece shown below. Tension can vary from person to person and yarn to yarn—if your piece is too long or too short, adapt the row count so that it matches the dimensions shown below. You might need to knit a few rows more or less than 218-220 rows to match the dimensions.

### STEP 2: SEAMING THE ENDS

You'll now have two pieces of knitting. Use a crochet hook to seam the ends closed. (See pages 14-15 for details). Remove the scrap yarn.

### STEP 3: SEAMING THE PIECES TOGETHER

Next, pull the two pieces together using stitch markers. Use the Mattress Stitch (see details on pages 22-23) to seam the two pieces together. Work two stitches at a time.

### STEP 4: ASSEMBLING THE BAG

If you're using a 46 needle machine, after you finish seaming your pieces, the final dimensions of the piece should be approximately 41" wide by 13" tall. If you use a 48 needle machine, the dimensions should be the same, but slightly larger.

# Large Tote Bags ...continued

When you finish seaming, lay your work flat. Fold the right corner down. Then, fold the left corner up. Bring the right corner up to make the shape above. Use stitch markers to pull the work together on both sides. Use a yarn tail from the middle of the work, thread it onto a darning needle and thread

it through the middle of the stitches to the center of the work and then secure with a knot on the inside of the bag.

Use the Mattress Stitch again to seam the sides together. When you reach the end, make sure to pick up all the last couple of stitches at the corner, so you don't end up with a hole in the corner. Then, thread the needle to the inside corner, secure with a few good knots and weave in the end into the center of the work and trim the yarn.

Turn over the work and repeat on the other side. When you finish, weave in any extra yarn tails.

### STEP 5: KNITTING THE HANDLE
Cast on to a 22 needle knitting machine using scrap yarn. **Knit 5 rows in the scrap yarn**. Switch to the main color, leaving a 1-2' tail. For the size handle shown in the photos, **knit 100 rows in the main color**. However, if you'd like the bag to sit a little higher, **knit less rows. For a shorter handle, knit 25-50 rows**. Switch back to the scrap yarn, leaving a long tail. **Knit 5 rows in the scrap yarn**. Cut the yarn and continue knitting until the work falls off the needles. Pull the work out of the machine and gently stretch out the stitches.

### STEP 6: SEAMING THE HANDLE ENDS
Use a crochet hook to seam the open ends of the handle. (See pages 14-15 for details).

### STEP 7: ATTACHING THE HANDLE
The sides of the bag are corners, so seam half of the handle edge to to the right side of the corner, and half of the handle edge to the left side of the corner. Thread one of the yarn tails onto a darning needle and begin by sewing one stitch through both beginning stitches to to secure the work. Then, switch to the Mattress Stitch, picking up 1 stitch at a time from the edges of each seam, and work back and forth until the end of the row.

Then, secure the last stitch by going all the way through both stitches. Secure with a knot and weave in and trim the ends. Repeat the same process on the other side of the handle.

The last step is to secure the edges of where we attached the handle. Cut a length of yarn in the main color and use a darning needle to sew through about 3-4 stitches on either side of where you attached the handle. Then, tie a tight knot with the two yarn tails on the inside of the bag. Secure with a couple more knots and weave in and trim the ends. Repeat the same process on the other handle. If desired, add a knitting tag. Your bag is now complete!

# Bow Headbands

This is one of the quicker projects in the book—knit on a 22 needle circular machine in two pieces, the pattern is adaptable to make the headband wider or smaller, and the bow wider or smaller.

## Supplies

- [ ] 22 needle circular knitting machine
- [ ] Weight 4/Medium yarn
- [ ] Crochet hook
- [ ] Darning needle
- [ ] Scissors
- [ ] Tape measure
- [ ] Knitting tag (optional)

## Quick Recipe

### MAIN PIECE:
- 22 needle knitting machine
- Cast on and off with scrap yarn
- Small: Knit 155 rows
- Medium: Knit 160 rows
- Large: Knit 165 rows
- Extra Large Bow: Knit 170 rows

### CENTER OF THE BOW:
- 22 needle knitting machine
- Cast on and off with scrap yarn
- All sizes: Knit 20 rows

### STEP 1: KNITTING THE MAIN PIECE
Cast on to a 22 needle circular knitting machine, using scrap yarn. **Knit 5 rows in the scrap yarn.** Switch to the main color yarn, leaving a long yarn tail to use for seaming later. **For the size small, knit 155 rows. For the size medium, knit 160 rows. For the size large, knit 165 rows.**

For an extra large sized bow, knit 170 rows. Switch back to scrap yarn. **Knit 5 rows in the scrap yarn.** Cut the yarn and continue knitting until the work falls off the needles. Pull the work out of the machine and gently stretch out the stitches. Set the work aside while you knit the center of the bow.

### STEP 2: KNITTING THE CENTER
Cast on to a 22 needle knitting machine using scrap yarn. **Knit 5 rows in the scrap yarn.** Switch to main color yarn. **For all sizes, knit 20 rows in the main color.** Switch back to scrap yarn. **Knit 5 rows in the scrap yarn.** Cut the yarn and continue knitting until the work falls off the needles. Pull the work out of the machine and gently stretch out the stitches.

### STEP 3: SEAMING THE ENDS
Use a crochet hook to seam the open ends of the tubes closed. (See pages 14-15 for details). Remove the scrap yarn.

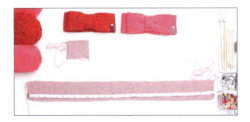

When the two pieces are finished and seamed, the headband piece will measure approximately 31.5" (size small), 32.5" (size medium), or 33.5" (size large). The center of the bow will measure approximately 3" tall x almost 4" wide.

### STEP 4: ASSEMBLING THE BOW
Lay out the headband flat. Fold the left side over, so that the section measures 3.5". Then, fold the right side over, so that section also measures 3.5". Then, pull the two sides together. The bow area should measure 7" and the headband itself should measure 8.5" wide for the small, 9" for the medium, and 9.5" for the large. If you're making the extra large size bow, make the sections wider— as wide as they need to be to keep the headband the desired size.

### STEP 5: JOINING THE HEADBAND
This is how the headband will look when it's folded, before it's seamed.

# Bow Headbands ...continued

Thread a yarn tail onto a darning needle and join the bow sides and the headband at the same time. You want to stitch together both the headband and the bow. Thread through one stitch from the edge of the top of the bow to the back of the bow. Then, thread the yarn through to the other side's back of the bow to connect the headband. Then, thread back to the top of the second side of the bow.

When stitching on the back side of the bow, make sure to stitch over the interior bars vertically—and not horizontally across the V-shaped stitches.

Make sure the seam under the bow looks nice, but don't worry too much about the seam looking perfect on the top, because you'll be covering that area with the center of the bow later. Continue until the end of the row, then secure with knots and weave in the ends.

When you finish seaming the sides together, this is how the project will look:

### STEP 6: ATTACHING THE CENTER OF THE BOW

Next, seam the two sides of the bow pieces together to create a tube. Use the Mattress Stitch to stitch through 2 bars on one side, followed by 2 bars on the other side, until the end of the row. Don't worry about making the seam look perfect, because it won't show in the final headband.

Tie the two yarn tails together to secure. Turn the headband inside out, and place the center of the headband with the seamed side facing the headband, around the back. It will feel dificult to pull together at first, but pull the sides around the headband tightly. Thread one of the yarn tails onto a darning needle, and thread through both sides of one of the V-shaped stitch on the top side, and pull the yarn through. Then, thread the yarn through both sides of one

of the V-shaped stitches on the bottom side, and pull the yarn through. Continue in this pattern, alternating between top and bottom stitches, pulling as tightly as you can without breaking the yarn, until the end of the row.

When you finish the seam, tie the two yarn tails together with a few good knots. Make sure to place the knots on the side of the center of the bow, not on the top, so that the knot doesn't sit against the forehead when worn. Thread the tail through the center of the bow back and forth a few times to hide the tail, and then trim the tail. Repeat with the other tail. Turn the headband right side out. If desired, add a knitting tag. Your bow headband is complete!

# WRISTLET CLUTCH

This wristlet clutch is perfect for when you're on the run—throw in just the basics: your phone, wallet and keys, and you're ready to go! Hand-knit or machine-knit the I-Cord wristlet, or mix it up with a crochet or braided handle.

## SUPPLIES

- [ ] 40 needle circular knitting machine
- [ ] Weight 4/Medium yarn
- [ ] 9" zipper
- [ ] Sewing kit
- [ ] Pins
- [ ] Double pointed knitting needles or I-Cord knitting machine
- [ ] Darning needle
- [ ] Scissors
- [ ] Stitch markers
- [ ] Knitting tag (optional)

## QUICK RECIPE

**BAG:**
- 40 needle machine
- Cast on and off with scrap yarn
- **Knit 102 rows**

- Graft the ends together
- Seam the bottom
- Sew in the zipper

**HANDLE:**
- Hand-knit or use an I-Cord machine to create a 13" I-Cord
- Attach to the zipper

### STEP 1: KNITTING THE BAG
Cast on to a 40 needle circular knitting machine using scrap yarn. **Knit 5 rows in the scrap yarn.** Switch to the main color, leaving a very long tail to use for seaming

the bag later. **Knit 102 rows in the main color.** Switch back to scrap yarn, leaving another long tail in the main color. **Knit 5 rows in the scrap yarn.** Cut the yarn and continue knitting until the work falls off the needles. Pull the work out of the machine and gently stretch out the stitches.

Keep in mind that tension varies from person to person and yarn to yarn—for this pattern, the goal is to knit a piece 19" long before seaming, or approximately 9.5" wide after the ends are grafted. Depending on your tension and yarn, you may need to knit a few more or less rows to achieve that measurment.

### STEP 2: GRAFTING THE ENDS
Graft the two open ends of the tube together. (See pages 18-19 for details). Remove the scrap yarn.

If there's a visible seam after you're done grafting, move the seam to the side of the bag, where it will be less visible. Secure the yarn tail with a knot and weave in the yarn tail to the center of the work.

### STEP 3: SEAMING THE BOTTOM
Use the Mattress Stitch to seam the bottom of the bag. (See pages 22-23 for details). Use stitch markers to pull the work together temporarily while you seam. Secure the yarn tail with a knot and weave in the yarn tail to the center of the work. If desired, add a knitting tag to the top of the bag.

# WRISTLET CLUTCH ...CONTINUED

## STEP 4: SEWING THE ZIPPER

Sew the zipper into the top of the bag (see page 25 for details). If you used a tag, sew right up to the tag, then thread through just the zipper fabric behind the tag, and then begin sewing again right after the tag. For a more secure zipper, sew two rows. As you sew, make sure you're stitching over the interior bars of the knitting, not over the V-shaped stitches. This will help ensure a cleaner seam.

For a stronger zipper, sew two rounds of stitches. When you're done, tie the thread securely under the zipper fabric.

## STEP 5: KNITTING THE I-CORD

For this project, you can create the wristlist in many ways. You can crochet the wristlet, use a faux leather wristlet, use an I-Cord knitting machine or you can hand-knit an I-Cord. The bag shown in the photos features a hand-knit I-Cord.

Cast on 4 stitches to two US Size 9 double pointed needles. Knit 4 stitches. When you finish the row, push the stitches to the right side of the needle (without turning the needle around). Use the working yarn from the back-left side of the work to knit. Knit 4 stitches.

Continue in this process, knitting 4 stitches, moving the stitches to the right and knitting the stitches using the working yarn from the back, until the work reaches approximately 13" long.

Bind off the stitches and secure with a knot. Thread your yarn onto a darning needle and stitch up the bottom a few times to round out the bottom of the I-Cord. Leave the yarn tails out, which we'll use later to attach the wristlet to the purse.

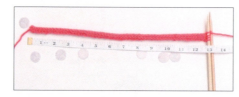

## STEP 5: ATTACHING THE I-CORD

Next, attach your wristlet cord to the zipper. If your darning needle is too large to fit through the zipper hole, use the pointy part of the darning needle to push one of the yarn tails through and pull it through with your hands. Then, push the other yarn tail through and tie it firmly with a few good knots.

Then, thread the tail onto the darning needle and work through a few of the stitches on the bottom of the cord to round out the shape. Then, secure with a knot and thread

the yarn through through the center of the I-Cord and trim the ends. Or, alternatively, if you prefer the wristlet to be attached directly to the bag, stitch the wristlet directly into the side corner of the bag.

You can customize the bag in many ways: you could line the bag with fabric, add an embellishment to the front, or you could knit the bag in two colors, with different colors on each side of the bag. Your wristlet clutch is complete!

# I-Cord Bracelets

One of the quickest patterns in the book—these bracelets make a great last-minute gift! They are both stylish and warm—the perfect winter accessory.

## Supplies

- [ ] I-Cord knitting machine
- [ ] Weight 3 Yarn
- [ ] 1.5" wide rhinestone buckle
- [ ] Darning needle
- [ ] Scissors
- [ ] Tape measure
- [ ] 1" Knitting tag

### Quick Recipe

**SMALL/MEDIUM:**
- Knit a 38" long I-Cord

**LARGE:**
- Knit a 43" long I-Cord

### SIZING

The small/medium bracelet measures approximately 8.5" in circumference. The large bracelet measures approximately 9.5" in circumference. This pattern is very adaptable in terms of sizing. Keep in mind that the I-Cords are fairly stretchy, so err on the side of smaller rather than larger.

### STEP 1: KNITTING THE I-CORD

Use an I-Cord knitting machine to knit an I-Cord—approximately **38" long for the size small/medium**, or **approximately 43" for the size large**. (See pages 26-27 for details on how to use an I-Cord machine).

Cast off the I-Cord, and bind off the end with a darning needle. Tighten up both ends with a few good knots.

### STEP 2: ASSEMBLING THE BRACELET

Thread the I-Cord through the buckle, placing the buckle in the middle of the I-Cord.

Continue wrapping the I-Cord around the buckle, threading the I-Cord up through one side, over the bar, and down through the other side, until you have five I-Cords wrapped over the buckle bar.

Use the two yarn tails from the ends of the I-Cord to tie a few strong knots between the two ends of the I-Cord, around the other four wraps of the bracelet.

For this project, I'm using a 1" tall knitting tag. Wrap it around the joined area of the I-Cord. Thread the shorter yarn tail onto a darning needle and weave it into the center of the I-Cord and trim the tail. With the longer yarn tail, sew the knitting tag around the I-Cord. When you finish sewing, secure the yarn tail with a knot on an interior bar of the I-Cord and thread the tail into the center of the I-Cord and trim the tail. Your bracelet is complete!

# SHOULDER PURSE

SIZING:
Approximately
11" wide x 6.75" tall

This shoulder purse is stylish, functional, and so customizable! You can use a faux leather handle as in the example, or you could switch it up and use a crochet, knit, braided or I-Cord handle.

## SUPPLIES

- ☐ 46 or 48 needle knitting machine
- ☐ Weight 4/Medium yarn
- ☐ Crochet hook
- ☐ Darning needle
- ☐ Scissors
- ☐ Sewing kit
- ☐ Pins
- ☐ Stitch markers
- ☐ 1" rings
- ☐ Purse handle
- ☐ 8" zipper
- ☐ Knitting tag (optiona)

### QUICK RECIPE

- 46 or 48 needle machine
- Cast on and off with scrap yarn
- **Knit 110 rows in main color**
- Graft the ends of the tubes together
- Use the Mattress Stitch to seam the bottom of the bag
- Sew in the rings
- Sew in the zipper
- Add the handles

### STEP 1: KNITTING THE MAIN PIECE
Cast on to a 46 or 48 needle circular knitting machine using scrap yarn. **Knit 5 rows in the scrap yarn.** Switch to the main color yarn. **Knit 110 rows in the main color.** Switch back to the scrap yarn. **Knit 5 rows in the scrap yarn.** Cut the yarn and continue knitting until the work falls off the needles. Pull the work out of the machine and gently stretch out the stitches.

### STEP 2: GRAFTING THE ENDS
Graft the ends of the tubes together (see details on pages 18-19) to create a tube. Remove the scrap yarn.

### STEP 3: SEAMING THE BOTTOM
Use stitch markers to bring together the bottom of the bag for support while seaming. Use the Mattress Stitch (details on page 22-23) to seam the bottom of the bag.

### STEP 5: SEW IN THE RINGS
Add the rings to the sides of the bags. Thread a length of yarn in the main color onto a darning needle and begin threading from the inside of the bag to the outside, leaving the yarn tail on the inside. When stitching the outside, stitch over the interior bars, not the exterior V-shaped stitches. Thread back and forth horizontally across the ring, capturing stitches on both outside areas of the ring, as well as the inside, to secure it in place. When it's secure, thread the yarn back to the inside, tie the two yarn tails with a knot and weave in and trim the ends. Repeat on the other side with the second ring.

### STEP 6: SEW IN THE ZIPPER:
If you're adding a knitting tag, add it before sewing the zipper. Sew the zipper into the top of the bag, between the two rings (see details on page 25). If you used a knitting tag, sew right up to the tag, then thread through just the zipper fabric, and begin as closely as possible again after the knitting tag.

If you have extra room on the sides of the zipper, use the main color yarn to stitch over the zipper fabric. Hook your purse handles onto the rings. Your bag is complete!

# CROSSBODY PHONE BAG

SIZING:
Approximately
4.5" wide x 7.5" tall

This is a very quick project—and so functional! A great bag for times where you only want to carry your phone, but don't need to keep your wallet and keys on hand.

## SUPPLIES

- ☐ 46 or 48 needle knitting machine
- ☐ I-Cord knitting machine
- ☐ Weight 4/Medium yarn
- ☐ Darning needle
- ☐ Scissors
- ☐ Knitting tag (optional)

### QUICK RECIPE

- 46 or 48 needle knitting machine
- Cast on and off with scrap yarn

**BAG:**
- Knit 42 rows

**HANDLE:**
- Knit a 42" I-Cord

### SIZING

This pattern is sized to fit a phone which measures approximately 3" wide x 6" tall. The bag measures approximately 4.5" wide x 7.5" tall. If your phone is larger, you can adjust the width by knitting more rows. A smaller phone will fit the pattern as written. The height will remain the same. The 48 needle machine will create a bag a touch higher than the 46 needle machine.

### STEP 1: KNITTING THE BAG

Cast on to a 46 or 48 needle circular knitting machine using scrap yarn. **Knit 5 rows in the scrap yarn.** Switch to your main color, leaving a long tail to use later when grafting the stitches together and seaming the bottom. **Knit 42 rows in the main color.** Switch back to the scrap yarn, leaving another long yarn tail. **Knit 5 rows in the scrap yarn.** Cut the yarn and continue knitting until the work falls off the needles. Pull the work out of the machine and gently stretch out the stitches.

### STEP 2: KNITTING THE HANDLE

This project includes an I-Cord handle. However, if you prefer, you can crochet, hand-knit, or braid the handle.

Cast on to an I-Cord knitting machine using the main color yarn. (See pages 26-27 for details). Knit a long I-Cord, at least 42" long. When you reach at least 42" (or you can knit a few extra inches to be on the safe side), cut an 8-10" tail in the yarn, unhook the needles and pull the work out of the machine.

Gently stretch out and untwist the I-Cord. The I-Cord will stretch a bit, so stretching it out before you measure it will help ensure a more accurate measurment. If you've knit longer than 42", gently pull the stitches out until the handle measures 42".

Thread the yarn tail onto a darning needle, pick up all 4 live stitches, and secure the end with a knot. Set aside the handle for now, while you seam and assemble the bag.

### STEP 3: GRAFTING THE ENDS TOGETHER

Graft the two ends of the bag together (see pages 18-19 for details). As you work, don't pull the yarn too tightly and make sure to keep an even tension.

When you reach the end of the seam, tie the two yarn tails with a knot, and remove the scrap yarn.

If your knot is noticable at the end of grafting, turn the work inside out and place that knot on the inside-bottom of the bag.

### STEP 4: SEAMING THE BOTTOM

Thread one of the yarn tails onto a darning needle and use the Mattress Stitch to seam the bottom of the bag closed. (See pages 22-23 for details). Make sure to follow along the same 2 rows of stitches as you work to ensure a clean seam.

When you reach the end, secure with one quick knot, and then thread the tail with a darning needle into the inside of the bag. Turn the bag inside out, secure the yarn tail with a few good knots and weave the yarn into the center of the work to hide the tail. Turn the work right side out.

### STEP 5: ATTACHING THE HANDLE

Next, attach the handles to the sides of the bag. Thread one of the yarn tails onto a darning needle, and work through 3 interior bars on one side of the bag.

Thread back through the I-Cord and then on the next round, thread through about 5 stitches, directly underneath the 3 previous stitches, and again back through the I-Cord. Next, continue sewing through a few stitches all around the bottom of the I-Cord and the side of the bag. This needs to be a

strong join, so make sure to work through a number of stitches all around to create a strong, secure join.

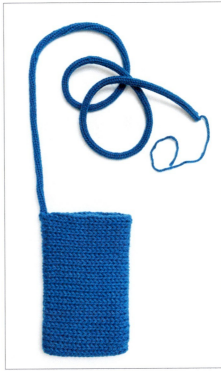

Before you attach the second side of the handle, untwist the I-Cord as much as possible. Then, repeat the same process as earlier to attach the second handle.

### STEP 6: FINAL TOUCHES

If desired, add a knitting tag to the top of the bag. If you prefer a closure, you can add a button closure or a clasp to the top. If you'd like some additional structure, you can line the inside of the bag with fabric. Your bag is complete!

# WIDE GEOMETRIC HANDBAG

This bag is a wider version of the Geometric Handbag pattern on page 34. Find a blank template on pages 118-119 to sketch out your own bag design!

## SUPPLIES

- ☐ 22 needle circular knitting machine
- ☐ Weight 4/Medium Yarn
- ☐ Darning needle
- ☐ Crochet hook
- ☐ Scissors
- ☐ I-Cord knitting machine
- ☐ Knitting tag (optional)

## QUICK RECIPE

- **22 needle knitting machine**
- **Cast on and off with scrap yarn**

### PIECE 1:
- Square 1: Knit 16 rows
- Square 2: Knit 16 rows

### PIECE 2:
- Square 1: Knit 16 rows
- Square 2: Knit 15 rows
- Square 3: Knit 15 rows
- Square 4: Knit 16 rows

### PIECE 3:
- Square 1: Knit 16 rows
- Square 2: Knit 15 rows
- Square 3: Knit 15 rows
- Square 4: Knit 15 rows
- Square 5: Knit 15 rows
- Square 6: Knit 16 rows

### PIECE 4:
- Square 1: Knit 16 rows
- Square 2: Knit 15 rows
- Square 3: Knit 15 rows
- Square 4: Knit 15 rows
- Square 5: Knit 16 rows

### PIECE 5:
- Square 1: Knit 16 rows
- Square 2: Knit 15 rows
- Square 3: Knit 15 rows
- Square 4: Knit 16 rows

### PIECE 6:
- Square 1: Knit 16 rows
- Square 2: Knit 15 rows
- Square 3: Knit 16 rows

### HANDLES:
- Knit two 14" I-Cords

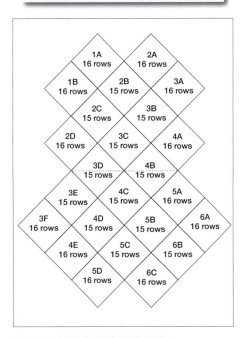

| | |
|---|---|
| 1A 16 rows | 2A 16 rows |
| 1B 16 rows | 2B 15 rows | 3A 16 rows |
| 2C 15 rows | 3B 15 rows |
| 2D 16 rows | 3C 15 rows | 4A 16 rows |
| 3D 15 rows | 4B 15 rows |
| 3E 15 rows | 4C 15 rows | 5A 16 rows |
| 3F 16 rows | 4D 15 rows | 5B 15 rows | 6A 16 rows |
| 4E 16 rows | 5C 15 rows | 6B 15 rows |
| 5D 16 rows | 6C 16 rows |

## STEP 1: DESIGNING THE HAT
Find the blank templates on pages 118-119 to sketch out the design of your bag.

## STEP 2: KNITTING THE BAG PIECES
Follow the graphic to the left, knitting 6 different pieces. Follow the chart from the top of each piece to the bottom. For instance, for Piece 2, you'll knit 2A, 2B, 2C, and finish with 2D.

As you knit, cast on before the first needle. However, **when you switch yarn colors (except for the cast on and cast off)**, **switch 3 needles after your desired row count.** This will "move" your yarn color changes to the inside of the bag, which will help create a cleaner seam. (More details on page 34).

**Piece 1:** Cast on to a 22 needle circular knitting machine using scrap yarn. **Knit 5 rows in the scrap yarn.** Switch to 1A's yarn color, leaving a long yarn tail to use later for seaming (as for all following cast ons). **Knit 16 rows in 1A's yarn.** Switch to 1B's yarn color. **Knit 16 rows in 1B's yarn.** Switch back to the scrap yarn. **Knit 5 rows in the scrap yarn.** Cut the yarn and continue knitting until the work falls off the needles.

**Piece 2:** Cast on to a 22 needle circular knitting machine using scrap yarn. **Knit 5 rows in the scrap yarn.** Switch to 2A's yarn color. **Knit 16 rows in 2A's yarn.** Switch to 2B's yarn color. **Knit 15 rows in 2B's yarn.** Switch to 2C's yarn color. **Knit 15 rows in 2C's yarn color.** Switch to 2D's yarn color. **Knit 16 rows in 2D's yarn color.** Switch back to the scrap yarn. **Knit 5 rows in the scrap yarn.** Cut the yarn and continue knitting until the work falls off the needles.

**Piece 3:** Cast on to a 22 needle circular knitting machine using scrap yarn. **Knit 5**

rows in the scrap yarn. Switch to 3A's yarn color. **Knit 16 rows in 3A's yarn.** Switch to 3B's yarn color. **Knit 15 rows in 3B's yarn.** Switch to 3C's yarn color. **Knit 15 rows in 3C's yarn color.** Switch to 3D's yarn color. **Knit 15 rows in 3D's yarn color.** Switch to 3E's yarn color. **Knit 15 rows in 3E's yarn color.** Switch to 3F's yarn color. **Knit 16 rows in 3F's yarn color.** Switch back to the scrap yarn. **Knit 5 rows in the scrap yarn.** Cut the yarn and continue knitting until the work falls off the needles.

**Piece 4:** Cast on to a 22 needle circular knitting machine using scrap yarn. **Knit 5 rows in the scrap yarn.** Switch to 4A's yarn color. **Knit 16 rows in 4A's yarn.** Switch to 4B's yarn color. **Knit 15 rows in 4B's yarn.** Switch to 4C's yarn color. **Knit 15 rows in 4C's yarn color.** Switch to 4D's yarn color. **Knit 15 rows in 4D's yarn color.** Switch to 4E's yarn color. **Knit 16 rows in 4E's yarn color.** Switch back to the scrap yarn. **Knit 5 rows in the scrap yarn.** Cut the yarn and continue knitting until the work falls off the needles.

**Piece 5:** Cast on to a 22 needle circular knitting machine using scrap yarn. **Knit 5 rows in the scrap yarn.** Switch to 5A's yarn color. **Knit 16 rows in 5A's yarn.** Switch to 5B's yarn color. **Knit 15 rows in 5B's yarn.** Switch to 5C's yarn color. **Knit 15 rows in 5C's yarn color.** Switch to 5D's yarn color. **Knit 16 rows in 5D's yarn color.** Switch back to the scrap yarn. **Knit 5 rows in the scrap yarn.** Cut the yarn and continue knitting until the work falls off the needles.

**Piece 6:** Cast on to a 22 needle circular knitting machine using scrap yarn. **Knit 5 rows in the scrap yarn.** Switch to 6A's yarn

color. **Knit 16 rows in 6A's yarn.** Switch to 6B's yarn color. **Knit 15 rows in 6B's yarn.** Switch to 6C's yarn color. **Knit 16 rows in 6C's yarn color.** Switch back to the scrap yarn. **Knit 5 rows in the scrap yarn.** Cut the yarn and continue knitting until the work falls off the needles.

### STEP 3: SEAMING THE ENDS
You'll now have 6 completed pieces of knitting. Use a crochet hook to seam the ends closed and remove the scrap yarn. (See pages 14-15 for details).

Next, line up the pieces in the same shape as in the graph on the previous page.

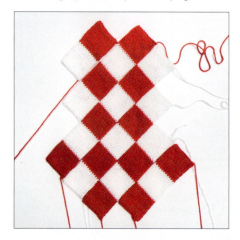

### STEP 4: SEAMING THE PIECES
Use the Mattress Stitch to seam the pieces together in the shape shown in the image. (See pages 22-23 for details).

### STEP 5: SEAMING THE BAG
Turn the work upside down and with the inside facing up. Fold the bottom up to the top. Then, fold in the side corners.

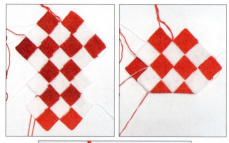

Use the Mattress Stitch to seam the pieces starting from the bottom and working your way to the top, leaving both sides of the top two corners un-seamed, as the opening of the bag.

### STEP 6: FINAL TOUCHES
Knit two 14" I-Cords and attach to the corners to make handles. If desired, add a knitting tag. Turn the bag inside out and secure all tails with knots and weave them into the center of the work and trim. Your bag is complete!

**SIZING:**
Approximately
9" wide x 3" tall

Perfect for back to school—these cases are great for pencils, pens, or even crochet hooks or double pointed knitting needles! The pom pom zippers add a touch of sweetness.

## Supplies

- [ ] 22 needle circular knitting machine
- [ ] Weight 4/Medium yarn
- [ ] 9" zipper
- [ ] Sewing kit
- [ ] Pins
- [ ] Pom pom maker
- [ ] Darning needle
- [ ] Scissors

### Quick Recipe

**BAG:**
- 22 needle knitting machine
- Cast on and off with scrap yarn
- **Knit 102 rows**

- Graft the ends together
- Seam the bottom
- Sew in the zipper
- Make and attach the pom pom

**NOTE:**
If you prefer a taller bag, you can knit this bag on a 40 needle circular knitting machine instead. Follow all the same directions.

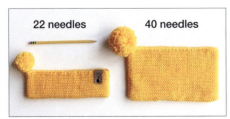

22 needles          40 needles

### STEP 1: KNITTING THE BAG
Cast on to a 22 needle circular knitting machine with scrap yarn. **Knit 5 rows in the scrap yarn.** Next, leave a very long tail in the main color yarn and **knit 102 rows in the main color.**

**Note:** Tension can vary from person to person and yarn to yarn. For this pattern, the goal is to create a piece that is 9"-9.5" inches wide after it's grafted. You may need to adjust the row count to a few rows more or less to achieve that width.

Switch back to the scrap yarn, leaving a long yarn tail in the main color. **Knit 5 rows in the scrap yarn.** Cut the scrap yarn and continue knitting until the work falls off the needles. Pull the work out of the machine and gently stretch out the stitches.

### STEP 2: GRAFTING THE ENDS
Graft the two open ends of the tube together. (See pages 18-19 for details). Remove the scrap yarn.

### STEP 3: SEAMING THE BOTTOM
Use the Mattress Stitch to seam the bottom of the bag, using the same row the entire seam. (See pages 22-23 for details). Secure the yarn tail with a knot and weave in the yarn tail to the center of the work.

### STEP 4: SEWING THE ZIPPER
If you're using a knitting tag, add it to the top of the bag now. Sew the zipper into the top of the bag (see page 25 for details). If you've used a tag, sew right up to the tag, then thread through just the zipper fabric behind the tag, and then begin sewing again right after the tag. For a more secure zipper, sew two rows.

### STEP 5: MAKING A POM POM
Use a pom pom maker to create a pom pom. (Or alternatively, you can DIY a pom pom in many ways—using cardboard, a fork, or your hands, for example). Leave two yarn tails from the pom pom. Next, attach the pom pom to the zipper. If your darning needle is too big to fit through the zipper hole, use the sharp part of a darning needle to push one of the yarn tails through. Then, push the other yarn tail through the other way. Then, secure the two yarn tails with a few good knots and trim the tail. Your bag is complete!

This pattern for a knit flower bouquet makes a lovely—and very low maintanence—gift. No watering nessesary! Plus, they are a great way to use up leftover yarn in a variety of colors!

# SUPPLIES

- [ ] 46 or 48 needle knitting machine
- [ ] 22 needle knitting machine
- [ ] Weight 4/Medium Yarn
- [ ] Flower vase
- [ ] Stuffing
- [ ] Crochet hook
- [ ] Darning needle
- [ ] Scissors
- [ ] Hair elastics
- [ ] Green pipe cleaners
- [ ] Stitch markers

*This project contains small parts, pipecleaners and a vase—**keep out of reach from children and babies***

## QUICK RECIPE

**PETALS:**
- 46 or 48 needle knitting machine
- Cast on and off with scrap yarn
- **Knit 20 rows**

**CENTER:**
- 22 needle knitting machine
- Cast on and off with main color
- **Knit 13 rows**

**STEM:**
- 46 or 48 needle knitting machine
- Cast on and off with scrap yarn
- **Knit 3 rows**

### STEP 1: KNITTING THE PETALS
Cast on to a 46 or 48 needle circular knitting machine using scrap yarn. **Knit 5 rows in the scrap yarn.** Switch to the color you're using for the flower petals (main color), leaving a long tail to use later when seaming. **Knit 20 rows in the main color.** Switch back to the scrap yarn, again leaving a long tail in the main color. **Knit 5 rows in the scrap yarn.** Cut the yarn and continue knitting until the work falls off the needles. Pull the work out of the machine and gently stretch out the stitches. Set the work aside for now, while you knit the center and stem.

### STEP 2: KNITTING THE STEM
Cast back on to the 46 or 48 needle knitting machine with scrap yarn. **Knit 5 rows in the scrap yarn.** Switch to a green yarn (or whatever color you prefer for the stem). **Knit 3 rows in the stem color.** Switch back to the scrap yarn. **Knit 5 rows in the scrap yarn.** Cut the yarn and continue knitting until the work falls off the needles. Pull the work out of the machine and gently stretch out the stitches. Set the work aside for now, while you knit the center.

### STEP 3: KNITTING THE CENTER
Cast on to a 22 needle knitting machine, using the color you'd like for the center of the flower (yellow, in the bouquet shown here). Do not use scrap yarn. **Knit 13 rows in the main color.** When you finish, cut a long tail in the main color and thread the yarn onto a darning needle. Use the darning needle to pick up all the stitches off the machine (similar to how you would cast off if you were making a hat). Use the top tail to cinch one side closed. You'll now have three pieces of knitting finished: the piece for the petals, the piece for the stem, and the piece for the center of the flower.

### STEP 4: ASSEMBLING THE PETALS
Turn the work inside out, with the V-shaped stitches on the inside. Scrunch up the work and wrap a hair elastic around the middle.

Line up the sides with the loops directly on top of each other and use a crochet hook to crochet the seam closed, beginning with the loops directly next to the yarn tails (similar to seaming a scrunchie). Start with the lower loop, and pull through the top loop. Then pull through the next top loop to the left. Then pull through the next bottom loop to the left. Continue in this pattern until you're 1.5" away from the end of the row.

When you're 1.5" away from the end, lightly fill the center of the work with stuffing. Don't over-stuff the work. A small amount is fine. Make sure to push it around so it is stuffed evenly. Then, finish seaming the edge, and pull your yarn tail through the last loop and secure with a knot.

# FLOWER BOUQUET ...CONTINUED

Tie the two yarn tails together to secure. You will now have a stuffed circle. Remove the scrap yarn. Choose which side will be your "front" and "back". The back will be where you add your knots. Use stitch markers to plan where you want to place your 5 indents (or cinches). As you're pulling the cinches, pull as tightly as you can, but not so tightly that your yarn breaks.

For the first cinch, your yarn will be at the top, so thread one of the yarn tails onto a darning needle and sew back and forth in a line down to the center of the flower. Pull it tight and then wrap the yarn once around the exterior of the flower, around the cinched area, to reinforce the cinch. Then pull tightly and tie a knot between a stitch or two in the inside ring.

Thread your yarn through the inside loops to the beginning of the next cinch. Tie a knot around 1 stitch, and then sew back and forth straight in a line to the stitch marker. When you get to the top, remove the stitch marker and make sure to capture one of the top exterior stitches. Then, thread your needle back through the center of the work, to the inside loop. Pull the yarn to cinch the work, and then wrap the yarn around the cinch once to reinforce the cinch. Then tie a knot in the inside area to secure the cinch. Repeat the same process on the remaining cinch areas, in order to create 5 petals. Secure the yarn tails with

knots and weave in and trim the yarn tails. Set aside the work for now as you seam the center and the stem.

## STEP 5: ASSEMBLING THE CENTER
Use a very small amount of stuffing to fill the center. Use the other tail to cinch the other side closed. Secure that closure with a knot. Thread the other yarn tail with a darning needle to the other side and secure the two tails together with a knot.

Then, push the center through the middle of the outside of the flower, and use the yarn tails and a darning needle to sew along the edges of the yellow center, and the inside ring of the flower, to secure the center to the middle. Weave in and trim the remaining yarn tails of both the flower and the center.

## STEP 6: ASSEMBLING THE STEM
Flatten the work, with the yarn tails all the way to the left side. Use a crochet hook to seam one side of the tube. (See pages 14-15 for details). When you reach the end of the row, pull the yarn tail through the last stitch and secure with a knot.

Turn the work over and if you are using pipe cleaners, fold 1 or 2 green pipe cleaners to fit inside the tube. Make sure to use green, as the color can show through when the stitches are stretched. **Do not use pipe cleaners if giving this flower to a baby or child.** Crochet the seam closed, like

the other side. When you're done, pull the yarn tail through the last loop, secure with a knot, and then tie the two yarn tails together.

Use the 2 yarn tails and a darning needle to sew the stem onto the back of the flower center. Weave in and trim your ends. Your flower is complete!

## STEP 7: ASSEMBLING THE BOUQUET
When you finish knitting your desired number of flowers, arrange them in your vase. The flowers will be a bit floppy, so you'll need to secure them to each other. Arrange all but one flower in a circle. Cut a length of yarn from each flower color, and use them to sew 2 stitches between the flower and the flower next to it. Leave a circle in the middle of the flowers.

When your circle of flowers are stitched together, add the final flower into the middle of the circle, and then secure that middle flower to a few of the exterior circle flowers. Weave in and trim the yarn tails from the stitches. Your bouquet is complete!

# Flower Headbands

These headbands will bring out the smiles—a big, bright flower is attached to a cozy cinched headband. The sizing is easily adaptable to be made for children or adults alike.

## Supplies

- ☐ 40 needle knitting machine
- ☐ 46 or 48 needle knitting machine
- ☐ 22 needle knitting machine
- ☐ Weight 4/Medium Yarn
- ☐ Hair elastics
- ☐ Crochet hook
- ☐ Darning needle
- ☐ Scissors
- ☐ Hair elastics
- ☐ Stuffing
- ☐ Knitting tag (optional)

## Quick Recipe

**HEADBAND:**
- 40 needle knitting machine
- Cast on and off with scrap yarn
- **Knit 90 rows**

**PETALS:**
- 46 or 48 needle knitting machine
- Cast on and off with scrap yarn
- **Knit 20 rows**

**CENTER:**
- 22 needle knitting machine
- Cast on and off with main color
- **Knit 13 rows**

### STEP 1: KNITTING THE HEADBAND
Cast on to a 40 needle circular knitting machine using scrap yarn. **Knit 5 rows in the scrap yarn.** Switch to the main color you're using for the headband, leaving a long tail to use for seaming later. **Knit 90 rows in the main color.** (For a larger headband, knit a few more rows. For a smaller headband, knit less rows). Switch back to the scrap yarn, leaving another long tail in the main color. **Knit 5 rows in the scrap yarn.** Cut the scrap yarn and continue knitting until the work falls off the needles. Pull the work out of the machine and gently stretch out the stitches.

### STEP 2: SEAMING THE HEADBAND
Thread one of the long yarn tails onto a darning needle. Line up the stitches from both open sides of the headband, and thread the needles through all 4 stitches that are lined up vertically. Pull the yarn through. Go back up through the next row of 4 vertical stitches. Pull the yarn through. Continue in this pattern until the end of the row. You don't need to pull the yarn tightly as you seam, you can tighten up the yarn at the end. Next, remove the scrap yarn.

Gently pull the yarn tail to cinch the headband tight in the middle. Turn the headband inside out and tie the two yarn tails together tightly a few times. Secure the yarn tails with a few knots and weave in the ends.

### STEP 3: CREATE THE FLOWER
Follow the directions on pages 74-77 to create the petals and center of a flower (skipping the stem). Leave two long yarn tails to use to attach the flower to the headband.

(Back side of the flower)

### STEP 4: ATTACHING THE FLOWER TO THE HEADBAND
Use the two long yarn tails from the flower to tie the flower around the cinched area of the headband. Secure the yarn tail with a few good knots and then secure the flower to the headband by threading through the actual flower a few times before securing with another knot on the inside and weave in the ends. If desired, add a knitting tag. Your flower headband is complete!

# Mini Purses

**SIZING:**
Approximately
5.5" wide x 5.5" tall

These miniature bags are so much fun to make. You can easily customize the outside of the bag using The Duplicate Stitch to create an initial, pattern or picture.

## Supplies

- [ ] 40 needle circular knitting machine
- [ ] Weight 4/Medium yarn
- [ ] Crochet hook
- [ ] Darning needle
- [ ] Scissors
- [ ] Small purse handles (approximately 3.5" wide)
- [ ] Knitting tag (optional)

### Quick Recipe

**MAIN PIECE:**
- 40 needle knitting machine
- Cast on and off with scrap yarn
- **Knit 75 rows**

**SIDES (KNIT 2):**
- 40 needle knitting machine
- Cast on and off with scrap yarn
- **Knit 7 rows**

### STEP 1: KNITTING THE MAIN PIECE
Cast on to a 40 needle circular knitting machine using scrap yarn. **Knit 5 rows in the scrap yarn.** Switch to your main color yarn, leaving a long tail to use later for seaming. **Knit 75 rows in the main color.** Switch back to the scrap yarn, again leaving a long tail in the main color to use later for seaming. **Knit 5 rows in the scrap yarn.** Then, cut the scrap yarn and continue knitting until the work falls off the needles. Pull the work out of the machine

and gently stretch out the stitches. Put the work aside for now while you knit the two side pieces.

### STEP 2: KNITTING THE SIDES
Cast on again to the 40 needle circular knitting machine using scrap yarn. **Knit 5 rows in the scrap yarn.** Switch to the main color yarn, leaving a long tail. **Knit 7 rows in the main color.** Switch back to the scrap yarn. **Knit 5 rows in the scrap yarn.** Cut the yarn and continue knitting until the work falls off the needles. Pull the work out of the machine and gently stretch out the stitches. If the cast on and cast off stitches are loose, pull the yarn tails gently to tighten them. Repeat the same process again to make the second side of the bag.

### STEP 3: SEAMING THE ENDS
You'll now have 3 pieces. Use a crochet hook to seam the ends closed. (See pages 14-15 for details). Remove the scrap yarn.

### STEP 4: SEWING THE BAG TOGETHER
Lay the main piece out flat, and place one of the purse handles at the top. Wrap the top over the handle. Add a few stitch markers to keep the work in place as you seam. Use a yarn tail and a darning needle to seam the work together. As you stitch through the exterior stitches, work over the interior bars of the stitches, not over the V-shaped stitches, to create a clean seam on the outside.

Repeat the same process on the other side of the bag, with the second purse handle.

## STEP 5: SEAMING THE SIDES

Place the first side in place next to the bag, with all the yarn tails on the inside of the bag. Thread the long yarn tail onto a darning needle, thread through the first couple of top stitches fully, a few times, to create a strong seam at the top of the bag. Then, secure the yarn with a knot on the inside of the bag, and use the Mattress Stitch to seam down the side of the bag. (See pages 22-23 for details). You can work one stitch at a time, or two stitches at a time.

When you get to the bottom, turn the corner and seam the bottom. Then, continue using the Mattress Stitch to seam the other side of the bag. Make sure to thread through the last couple of stitches a few times, to ensure a strong join. Then, secure the yarn tail with a knot on the inside of the purse. You can leave all the yarn tails loose in the bag for now, as we'll come back later to secure and weave them in.

Repeat the same process on the other side of the bag, with the second side piece.

## STEP 6: WEAVING IN THE ENDS

Turn the bag inside out. Trim the yarn tails and secure them all with knots. Then, thread the tails onto a darning needle and weave them into the center area to hide the yarn tails. Turn the bag right side out.

## STEP 7: FINAL TOUCHES

If desired, add a knitting tag to the side of the bag. **Note: This project is not intended for use by small children or infants.**

There are many ways to customize these bags. You could crochet, hand-knit or braid the handles. You could use an I-Cord machine or hand-knit an I-Cord for the handles. You could use double knitting to add an initial, pattern, or picture to the outside of the bag. Or, you could knit up a small pocket for the interior of the bag. Your bag is complete!

# Rainbow Hat

**SIZING:** Approximately 7.5" wide x 10.5" tall

This hat will put a smile on your face during the cold winter months! Switch up the pattern by using black instead of beige, or by playing with different colors in the stripes.

## Supplies

- [ ] 48 needle knitting machine
- [ ] Weight 4/Medium yarn
- [ ] Darning needle
- [ ] Scissors
- [ ] Pom pom
- [ ] Knitting tag (optional)

## Quick Recipe

### HAT:
48 needle knitting machine
Cast on and off with main color
- Knit 64 rows in main color (beige)
- Knit 2 rows in red
- Knit 2 rows in main color
- Knit 2 rows in orange
- Knit 2 rows in main color
- Knit 2 rows in yellow
- Knit 2 rows in main color
- Knit 2 rows in green
- Knit 2 rows in main color
- Knit 2 rows in blue
- Knit 2 rows in main color
- Knit 2 rows in purple
- Knit 24 rows in main color

### STEP 1: KNITTING THE HAT
Cast on to a 48 needle circular knitting machine using the main color of the hat. (Do not use scrap yarn). **Knit 64 rows in the main color** (beige, in the example shown to the right. Switch to the red. **Knit 2 rows in red.** Switch back to beige. **Knit**

2 row in beige. Knit 2 rows in orange. Knit 2 rows in beige. Knit 2 rows in yellow. Knit 2 rows in beige. Knit 2 rows in green. Knit 2 rows in beige. Knit 2 rows in blue. Knit 2 rows in beige. Knit 2 rows in purple. Switch back to the beige. **Knit 24 rows in beige.** Leave a very long yarn tail when you cut the yarn.

### STEP 2: CASTING OFF THE STITCHES
Thread the long yarn tail onto a darning needle and pick up all the stitches off the machine. (See pages 16-17 for details).

### STEP 3: SECURE THE YARN TAILS
Turn the work inside out. Secure any yarn tails with a few good knots.

### STEP 4: ASSEMBLING THE HAT
Use the yarn tail to cinch the bottom of the hat. As you're working, push the work inside if it begins to curl out. Tie a couple of knots to secure the cinch. Thread that tail onto a darning needle and push it through as you bring the bottom of the hat to meet the top of the hat. (See pages 28-29 for details).

With both yarn tails out at the top of the hat, cinch the top of the hat closed over the bottom. Tie the two yarn tails tightly to secure the top of the hat.

### STEP 5: WEAVE IN THE ENDS
Thread the yarn tails onto darning needles and weave the ends into the center areas of the work.

### STEP 5: FINAL TOUCHES
If desired, add a pom pom to the top of the hat, and a knitting tag to the bottom of the hat. If using a pom pom, make sure to tie it well to the top of the hat, a few different times, to ensure that it is secured well. Your rainbow hat is complete!

# Throw Pillow

**SIZING:**
Approximately
15" wide x 7" tall

This throw pillow will brighten any room! Adjust the colors depending on the season, for a spring, summer, fall, or winter pillow. Or, use school colors or sports colors to decorate your couch when watching your favorite games.

## Supplies

- [ ] 46 or 48 needle knitting machine
- [ ] Weight 4/Medium Yarn
- [ ] Crochet hook
- [ ] Darning needle
- [ ] Scissors
- [ ] Stuffing
- [ ] Knitting tag (optional)

### Quick Recipe

**EXTERIOR:**
46 or 48 needle knitting machine
Cast on and off with scrap yarn
- Stripe 1: Knit 14 rows
- Stripe 2: Knit 13 rows
- Stripe 3: Knit 13 rows
- Stripe 4: Knit 13 rows
- Stripe 5: Knit 13 rows
- Stripe 6: Knit 14 rows

**INTERIOR:**
46 or 48 needle knitting machine
Cast on and off with scrap yarn
- Knit 78 rows

### STEP 1: KNITTING THE PIECES
This throw pillow is knit in two pieces. For the exterior piece, cast on to a 46 or 48 needle circular knitting machine using scrap yarn. **Knit 5 rows in the scrap yarn.** Choose 6 colors for your stripes. **Knit 14 rows in the first color. Knit 13 rows in the second color. Knit 13 rows in the third color. Knit 13 rows in the fourth color. Knit 13 rows in the fifth color. Knit 14 rows in**

the sixth color. Switch back to the scrap yarn. **Knit 5 rows in the scrap yarn.** Cut the scrap yarn and continue knitting until the work falls off the needles.

For the interior, cast on to the same machine with scrap yarn. **Knit 5 rows in the scrap yarn.** Switch to a color for the interior layer. Ideally choose a color that doesn't contrast too strongly with your exterior colors (I chose beige in the example below), in case you can see it through any of the stitches. **Knit 78 rows in the interior color.** Switch back to the scrap yarn. **Knit 5 rows in the scrap yarn.** Cut the yarn and continue knitting until the work falls off the needles.

### STEP 2: SEAMING THE FIRST ENDS
Use a crochet hook to seam one end closed (see details on pages 14-15) on the exterior piece, and one end closed on the interior piece. Remove the scrap yarn from those two ends. Leave the other ends open. Place the interior piece inside the exterior piece.

### STEP 3: STUFFING THE PILLOW
Gently add stuffing to the interior piece.

When you finish stuffing the pillow, use a crochet hook to seam the interior pillow closed. Remove the scrap yarn.

Next, use a crochet hook to seam the exterior layer closed. Remove the scrap yarn. Secure the yarn tails with knots and weave in the ends. If desired, add a knitting tag to the side of the pillow. Your pillow is complete!

# Checkered Blanket

Knitting a blanket on a circular knitting machine is a big project, but well worth effort when you feel how cozy and warm they are! Find a blank template on pages 120-121 to sketch out your own design!

## Supplies

- [ ] 46 needle Addi® Express Kingsize
- [ ] Weight 4/Medium Yarn
- [ ] Crochet hook
- [ ] Darning needle
- [ ] Scissors
- [ ] Knitting tag (optional)

## Quick Recipe

### BLANKET PIECES (KNIT 6):
46 needle Addi knitting machine
Cast on and off with main color
- Square 1: Knit 33 rows
- Square 2: Knit 32 rows
- Square 3: Knit 32 rows
- Square 4: Knit 32 rows
- Square 5: Knit 32 rows
- Square 6: Knit 32 rows
- Square 7: Knit 32 rows
- Square 8: Knit 32 rows
- Square 9: Knit 33 rows

### A NOTE ABOUT TENSION
The goal for this blanket is for each section to be **square**. Tension can vary from person to person—so knit a test square before starting this project, and if you need to knit more or less rows to create a square shape, adapt the pattern accordingly. If you choose to knit more or less rows, make sure to **add one additional row to your first and last squares**. For instance, if you'll be knitting 33 rows per square, knit 34 rows for the first and last squares.

|   | A | B | C | D | E | F |
|---|----|----|----|----|----|----|
| 1 | 33 | 33 | 33 | 33 | 33 | 33 |
| 2 | 32 | 32 | 32 | 32 | 32 | 32 |
| 3 | 32 | 32 | 32 | 32 | 32 | 32 |
| 4 | 32 | 32 | 32 | 32 | 32 | 32 |
| 5 | 32 | 32 | 32 | 32 | 32 | 32 |
| 6 | 32 | 32 | 32 | 32 | 32 | 32 |
| 7 | 32 | 32 | 32 | 32 | 32 | 32 |
| 8 | 32 | 32 | 32 | 32 | 32 | 32 |
| 9 | 33 | 33 | 33 | 33 | 33 | 33 |

### STEP 1: DESIGNING THE BLANKET
Find the blank templates on pages 120-121. Use markers, crayons or colored pencils to sketch out your own design for the blanket.

### STEP 2: KNITTING THE BLANKET
Follow the graph above, knitting **6 pieces**: pieces A, B, C, D, E and F. Follow each piece from square 1 to square 9. Cast on to a 46 needle circular knitting machine using scrap yarn. **Knit 5 rows in the scrap yarn.** Switch to the Square 1 yarn color, leaving an approximately 10' yarn tail, to use later when seaming the blanket together. **Cast on to the right of the first needle.**

**Knit 33 rows for Square 1.** After you reach row 33, **knit three additional needles after you reach the needle where you cast on.** Then, cut a 5 or 6" tail in the yarn and throw it in the middle of the machine, **to the left of the third needle.** For all interior yarn color changes (all yarn color changes except for the scrap yarn changes), continue switching colors to the left of the 3rd needle. This will "move" the yarn color changes to the back of the blanket, which will help create a cleaner seam. Approximately 5 rows after each yarn color change, tie one quick temporary knot between the yarn tails.

**Knit 32 rows in the yarn color for Square 2.**
**Knit 32 rows in the yarn color for Square 3.**
**Knit 32 rows in the yarn color for Square 4.**
**Knit 32 rows in the yarn color for Square 5.**
**Knit 32 rows in the yarn color for Square 6.**
**Knit 32 rows in the yarn color for Square 7.**
**Knit 32 rows in the yarn color for Square 8.**

When the work starts to touch the table (likely at the beginning of Square 3) begin to roll the work up inside the machine. Continue rolling the work as you knit the entire piece.

When you finish row 32 for Square 8, switch to the yarn color for Square 9. **Knit 33 rows for Square 9, finishing the row to the right of the first needle (the same needle where you cast on the piece).** Leave another long tail, approximately 10' long, in the Square 9 yarn color, to use when seaming the blanket together, and switch back to the scrap yarn. **Knit 5 rows in the scrap yarn.** Cut the yarn, and continue knitting until the work falls off the needles. Pull the work out of the machine.

Repeat the process **5 more times**, to knit pieces B, C, D, E and F.

### STEP 3: FINALIZING THE KNOTS
Turn the work inside out. Secure all the yarn tails with a few good knots, checking the outside of the work as you knot them, to make sure you're tying tight enough to bring the stitches together, but not so tight that you bunch up the work. **Do not tie knots**

**between the scrap yarn and the cast on tail, or the scrap yarn and the cast off tail.** Trim the tails and turn the work right side out again.

### STEP 5: SEAMING THE ENDS
Use a crochet hook to seam the open ends of the tubes closed. (See pages 14-15 for details). Remove the scrap yarn.

### STEP 6: SEAMING THE PIECES TOGETHER
Line up two of the pieces together. Use stitch markers to pull the pieces together. One stitch marker per square works well. As you line up the tubes, try to identify one line of V-shaped stitches that runs all the

way from the top to the bottom, on either side, to seam together. And place the stitch markers directly under the lines you'll be seaming together.

Use the Mattress Stitch to seam the pieces together. (See pages 22-23 for details). As you work, thread through 2 bars at a time to speed things up. For a clean seam, make sure to stay within the same line of V-shaped stitches from beginning to end.

Repeat this process to seam together all 6 pieces of the blanket.

### STEP 6: FINAL TOUCHES
When you finish seaming the pieces, secure the yarn tails with a few good knots and then weave in the ends into the center of the work and trim the ends. If desired, you can also knit a border with a 22 needle circular knitting machine, and attach with the Mattress Stitch. If desired, add a knitting tag. Your blanket is complete!

# Boat Tote

**SIZING:**
Approximately
12.5" wide x 12.5" tall
(without the handle)

This "boat tote" is as cozy as it is functional! The handle is knit in a long tube—you'll want to set up your 22 needle machine between two tables, so the work can fall freely below the machine.

## Supplies

- [ ] 46 or 48 needle knitting machine
- [ ] 22 needle knitting machine
- [ ] Weight 4/Medium Yarn
- [ ] Crochet hook
- [ ] Darning needle
- [ ] Scissors
- [ ] Stitch markers
- [ ] Knitting tag (optional)

### Quick Recipe

**MAIN PIECES (KNIT 2):**
- 46 or 48 needle knitting machine
- Cast on and off with scrap yarn
- **Knit 140 rows**

**HANDLE:**
- 22 needle knitting machine
- Cast on and off with scrap yarn
- **Knit 400 rows**

### STEP 1: KNITTING THE MAIN PIECES

Cast on to a 46 or 48 needle circular knitting machine using scrap yarn. **Knit 5 rows in the scrap yarn.** Switch to the main color yarn (beige, in the example shown in the photo), leaving a long yarn tail to use later when seaming the bag together. **Knit 140 rows in the main color.** Switch back to the scap yarn. **Knit 5 rows in the scrap yarn.** Cut the yarn and continue knitting until the work falls off the needles. Pull the work off the machine and gently stretch out the stitches.

**Repeat the entire process again to create the second piece.**

### STEP 2: KNITTING THE HANDLE

Cast on to a 22 needle circular knitting machine using scrap yarn. For this project, set up the machine between two tables of the same height, so that the work can fall down in the middle of the tables (see example on page 24). **Knit 5 rows in the scrap yarn.** Switch to the handle color yarn (magenta, in the example shown in the photo), leaving a long yarn tail to use later when grafting the ends together. **Knit 400 rows in the handle color yarn.** Switch back to the scrap yarn. **Knit 5 rows in the scrap yarn.** Cut the yarn and continue knitting until the work falls off the needles. Pull the work off the machine and gently stretch out the stitches.

You'll now have **three pieces**: two main pieces and one long handle piece.

### STEP 3: SEAMING THE ENDS OF THE MAIN PIECES

Use a crochet hook to seam the ends closed from all four sides of the two main pieces (See pages 14-15 for details). **Do not seam the sides of the handles.** Remove the scrap yarn.

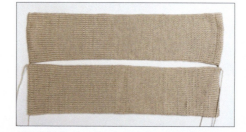

### STEP 4: GRAFTING THE ENDS OF THE HANDLE

Thread one of the yarn tails onto a darning needle and graft the ends of the tube together. (See pages 18-19 for details). Remove the scrap yarn.

### STEP 5: SEAMING THE MAIN PIECES

Thread one of the long yarn tails onto a darning needle and use the Mattress Stitch to seam the two main pieces together. (See details on pages 22-23). When you're done, weave in and trim the yarn tails into the center of the work.

## STEP 5: ASSEMBLING THE BAG

Lay the handle piece over the main piece of the bag. Make sure it's centered so that the handles on the top and bottom are the same size. For the bag shown in the example, the handles were seamed approximately 1.5" in from either side.

When you get to the top sides of the bags, seam the handle closed on the inside, using the seaming method on page 23. This will seam the handles fully to the bag, without an opening at the top.

Cut a long length in the handle color yarn and secure the yarn with a knot on the inside of the handle. Use the Mattress Stitch (see details on pages 22-23) to seam the sides of the handles to the bag, picking up two interior bar stitches from the handle, and then two interior bar stitches from the bag. Make sure you follow the same row the entire way through.

Use the Mattress Stitch to seam the sides of the bag. When you reach the ends, thread the yarn tails into the inside corners, secure with knots and weave in the ends. If desired, add a knitting tag to the top-center of the bag, where you joined the two main pieces together. Your bag is complete!

## STEP 6: SEAMING THE SIDES

You'll now have the handles seamed to the outside of the main pieces of the bag. Next, turn the work with the inside facing up. Then, fold it in half.

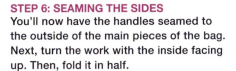

SIZING:
Approximately
18" wide x 20" tall
(with the handle)

# Travel Tote

This tote is simple to knit up and assemble—and great for on the go when you need to bring a few items. Find a blank template on page 132-133 to sketch out and design your own bag designs!

## Supplies

- [ ] 46 needle Addi® Express Kingsize
- [ ] I-Cord knitting machine
- [ ] Weight 4/Medium Yarn
- [ ] Crochet hook
- [ ] Darning needle
- [ ] Scissors
- [ ] Stitch markers
- [ ] Knitting tag (optional)

## Quick Recipe

- 46 needle knitting machine
- Cast on and off with scrap yarn

**PIECE 1:**
- Knit 66 rows

**PIECE 2:**
- Knit 98 rows

**PIECE 3:**
- Knit 130 rows

**PIECE 4:**
- Knit 34 rows

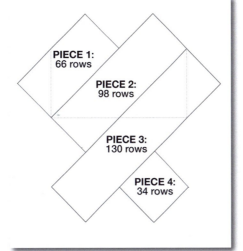

PIECE 1: 66 rows

PIECE 2: 98 rows

PIECE 3: 130 rows

PIECE 4: 34 rows

### STEP 1: KNITTING THE PIECES

**Piece 1:** Cast on to a 46 needle circular knitting machine with scrap yarn. **Knit 5 rows in the scrap yarn.** Switch to the main color, leaving a long tail to use for seaming later. **Knit 66 rows in the main color.** Switch back to the scrap yarn, again leaving a long tail to use for seaming later (and continue leaving long tails for casting on and off of the remaining pieces as well). **Knit 5 rows in the scrap yarn.** Cut the yarn and continue knitting until the work falls off the needles. Pull the work out of the machine and gently stretch out the stitches.

**Piece 2:** Cast on to a 46 needle circular knitting machine. **Knit 5 rows in the scrap yarn. Knit 98 rows in the main color. Knit 5 rows in the scrap yarn.** Cut the scrap yarn and continue knitting until the work falls off the needles.

**Piece 3:** Cast on to a 46 needle circular knitting machine. **Knit 5 rows in the scrap yarn. Knit 130 rows in the main color. Knit 5 rows in the scrap yarn.** Cut the scrap yarn and continue knitting until the work falls off the needles.

**Piece 4:** Cast on to a 46 needle circular knitting machine. **Knit 5 rows in the scrap yarn. Knit 34 rows in the main color. Knit 5 rows in the scrap yarn.** Cut the scrap yarn and continue knitting until the work falls off the needles.

**Note:** Tension can vary from person to person and yarn to yarn, so you may need to knit a few more or less rows to achieve the same dimensions. The goal is to match the dimensions shown in the diagram to the left, not nessesarily the exact row counts. Piece 1 should be 2x the length of Piece 4. Piece 2 should be 3x the length of Piece 4. And Piece 3 should be 4x the length of Piece 4.

### STEP 2: SEAMING THE ENDS

Use a crochet hook to seam the ends closed. (See pages 14-15 for details). Remove the scrap yarn. Lay the pieces out in the same shape as the diagram to the left.

# Travel Tote ...continued

If the long yarn tails are getting tangled, you can roll them into a small yarn ball and secure with a stitch marker.

### STEP 3: SEAMING THE PIECES
Use the Mattress Stitch to seam Piece 1 to Piece 2. (See details about the Mattress Stitch on pages 22-23).

Then, seam Piece 2 to Piece 3. Finally, seam Piece 4 to Piece 3. If it helps, pull the pieces together with a few stitch markers before you seam. When you seam Piece 4, make sure it's placed exactly in the position shown in the diagram.

As you work, make sure you're seaming along the exact same row of V-shaped stitches from beginning to end, to ensure a clean seam. As you finish your rows, secure the yarn tails with knots on the side of the piece that will be the inside of your bag.

### STEP 4: SEAMING THE BAG
Lay the seamed piece with the inside facing up. Bring the bottom up to meet the top.

Then, fold the left and right sides in.

Use the Mattress Stitch to seam the sides of the bag, working from the bottom to the top. (See pages 22-23 for details). As you seam the horizontal edges, make sure not to pull the yarn too tightly as you seam. You'll essentially be making a new stitch, so you'll want the tension to be approxiately similar to the knit stitches above and below.

### STEP 5: ADDING THE HANDLE
Use an I-Cord knitting machine to knit the handle. (See details on pages 26-27). The I-Cord handles shown in the photos here measure approximately 18" each, but you can adjust the handle length as desired. If you don't have an I-Cord knitting machine, you can hand-knit an I-Cord, or crochet or braid the handle instead. When the handles are complete, use a darning needle to attach them securely to the top corners.

### STEP 6: FINAL TOUCHES
Turn the bag inside out. Secure all the yarn tails with knots and weave the ends into the center of the knitting. Add a knitting tag, if desired. Your bag is complete!

# Triangle Tote

SIZING: Approximately 9.5" wide x 14" tall (with the handle)

This pattern is super simple—knit up three squares, seam them together, and you have a tote! Get creative with various colors, handles, and handle lengths. Find a blank template on pages 126-127 to design your own bag!

## Supplies

- [ ] 46 needle Addi® Express Kingsize
- [ ] Weight 4/Medium yarn
- [ ] Crochet hook
- [ ] Darning needle
- [ ] Scissors
- [ ] I-Cord knitting machine (optional)
- [ ] Knitting tag (optional)

## Quick Recipe

**MAIN PIECES (KNIT 3):**
46 needle circular knitting machine
Cast on and off with scrap yarn

- Knit 5 rows in the scrap yarn
- Knit 34 rows
- Knit 5 rows in the scrap yarn

**HANDLE:**
Knit an I-Cord: **15" long**

### NOTE:
The goal for this pattern is to knit 3 squares. Tension can vary from person to person, so you may need to knit one or two more or less rows than listed in the to achieve a square dimension based on your own personal tension and yarn.

### STEP 1: KNITTING THE PIECES
Cast on to a 46 needle circular knitting machine, using scrap yarn. **Knit 5 rows in the scrap yarn**. Switch to the first triangle color yarn. **Knit 34 rows in the main color.** Switch back to the scrap yarn. **Knit 5 rows in the scrap yarn.** Cut the yarn and continue knitting until the work falls off the needles. Pull the work out of the machine and gently stretch out the stitches.

Repeat the same process two more times, to create **three square pieces.**

### STEP 2: SEAMING THE ENDS
Use a crochet hook to seam the ends closed on all three pieces. (See pages 14-15 for details). Remove the scrap yarn.

### STEP 3: SEAMING THE PIECES
Place the three pieces as shown above. Use the Mattress Stitch to seam the pieces together. (See pages 22-23 for details).

### STEP 4: SEAMING THE BAG
Fold the left corner in. Then, fold the right corner in. Then, folder the bottom corner up. Use the Mattress Stitch to seam the sides together. Don't stitch too tightly when

seaming the horizontal sides together. You'll essentially be creating a new row of stitches, so keep the tension similar to the knit stitches above and below.

### STEP 5: KNITTING THE HANDLE
Use an I-Cord knitting machine to knit a 15" handle. (See details on pages 26-27). Or, knit a longer handle to create a crossbody bag. If you don't have an I-Cord machine, hand-knit or crochet the handle. Attach it securely to the corners using a darning needle.

### STEP 6: FINAL TOUCHES
Secure all remaining yarn tails with knots and weave them into the center of the work. If desired, add a knitting tag. Your bag is complete!

# Design-Your-Own-Hat Activity

Ask a child to sketch a hat design, and then follow their pattern to bring their idea to life! Find the blank coloring pages on pages 122-123.

## Supplies

- [ ] 46 or 48 needle knitting machine
- [ ] Weight 4/Medium Yarn
- [ ] Darning needle
- [ ] Scissors
- [ ] Pom pom maker (optional)
- [ ] Knitting tag (optional)

### Quick Recipe

**HAT:**
46 or 48 needle knitting machine
Cast on and off with main color
- Interior color: Knit 55 rows
- Then, follow pattern from the bottom to the top.
- 1st stripe: Knit 10 rows
- 2nd stripe: Knit 5 rows
- 3rd stripe: Knit 5 rows
- 4th stripe: Knit 5 rows
- 5th stripe: Knit 5 rows
- 6th stripe: Knit 5 rows
- 7th stripe: Knit 5 rows
- 8th stripe: Knit 5 rows
- 9th stripe: Knit 5 rows
- 10th stripe: Knit 5 rows
Total: 110 rows

### STEP 1: DESIGNING THE HAT
Find the blank coloring pages on pages 122-123 of this book. Ask a child to design their own hat, using markers, crayons, or paints. If the child doesn't stay within the lines, it's totally fine! Get creative and think of your own way to interpret their designs with your knitting.

### STEP 2: KNITTING THE HAT
Choose a color for the interior layer of the hat. Cast on to a 46 or 48 needle circular knitting machine using the interior color. (Do not cast on with scrap yarn). **Knit 55 rows in the interior color.**

Next, follow the coloring page from the bottom to the top. For the bottom stripe, which will be the brim, **knit 10 rows.** Then, **knit 5 rows each for all the remaining 10 stripes, for a total of 110 rows.**

When you finish the last stripe, cut a long tail in the yarn and use a darning needle to pick up all the stitches off the machine (see pages 16-17 for details).

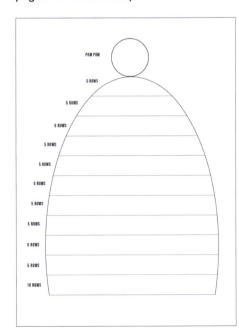

### STEP 3: ASSEMBLING THE HAT
Turn the piece inside out. Secure all the yarn tails from the yarn color changes with a few good knots. Check the tension on the exterior of the hat to make sure you're tying the knots tightly enough, but not too tight.

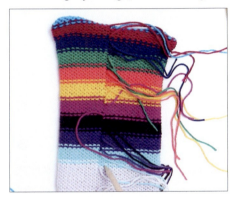

Use the yarn tail to cinch the bottom of the hat. As you're working, push the work inside if it begins to curl out. Tie a couple of knots to secure the cinch. Thread that tail onto a darning needle and push it through as you bring the bottom of the hat to meet the top of the hat. With both yarn tails out at the top of the hat, cinch the top of the hat closed over the bottom. Tie the two yarn tails tightly to secure the top of the hat and weave them in to the center of the work. (See details on pages 28-29).

### STEP 4: FINAL TOUCHES
Make a pom pom to match the design and attach it to the hat. If desired, add a knitting tag to the bottom of the hat. **Note: if giving this item to a child, do not use any potentially removable pieces.** Your hat is complete!

# Design-Your-Own-Scarf Activity

**SIZING:** Approximately 5" wide x 84" tall

A children's project to inspire creativity and design! Find the coloring pages on pages 124-125 of this book—follow the template to bring their ideas to life!

## Supplies

- [ ] 40 needle knitting machine
- [ ] Weight 4/Medium yarn
- [ ] Crochet hook
- [ ] Darning needle
- [ ] Scissors
- [ ] Book or other flat item to make the fringe
- [ ] Knitting tag (optional)

### Quick Recipe

**SCARF:**
40 needle circular knitting machine
Cast on and off with scrap yarn

- Knit 5 rows in the scrap yarn
- Knit 20 rows per stripe
- Knit 5 rows in the scrap yarn

**Total:** 20 stripes = 400 rows

### SIZING NOTE:
This scarf is **not intended for use by small children or infants.**

This pattern makes a long scarf. If you prefer a shorter scarf, you can adapt the pattern in two different ways: either knit less rows per stripe (for example, knitting 16 or 18 rows per stripe instead of 20 rows). Or, knit fewer stripes (for example: knit 15 stripes, for a total of 300 rows).

### STEP 1: DESIGNING THE SCARF
Find the blank coloring pages on pages 124-125 of this book. Ask a child to design their own scarf, using markers, crayons, colored pencils or paints.

### STEP 2: KNITTING THE SCARF
Cast on to a 40 needle circular knitting machine using scrap yarn. **Knit 5 rows in the scrap yarn.** Follow the designed template from one side of the scarf to the other. **Knit 20 rows per stripe, for a total of 20 stripes, and 400 rows.** As you work, continue to roll the work up inside the machine. Or, alternatively, set up your machine between two tables so that the work will fall under the table as you knit. (See photo on page 24). Switch back to the scrap yarn. **Knit 5 rows in the scrap yarn.** Cut the yarn and continue knitting until the work falls off the needles.

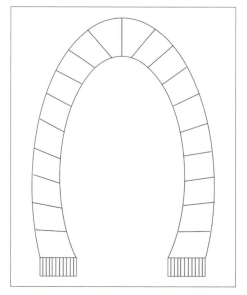

### STEP 3: SECURING THE YARN TAILS
Turn the tube inside out. You will have a large number of yarn tails from all the color changes. Secure all the yarn tails with a few good knots and trim the ends. Turn the work right side out.

### STEP 4: SEAM THE ENDS
Use a crochet hook to seam the ends of the scarf closed. (See pages 14-15 for details).

### STEP 5: ADD THE FRINGE
Wrap the fringe color yarn around a flat object, such as a book, numerous times. Cut along the length of the book, to leave you with a pile of similarly sized lengths of yarn. Grab 3 lengths of yarn at a time, and use a crochet hook to go through a stitch on the scarf edge, and grab the center of the lengths. Use your fingers to pull the yarn tails through the loop and pull it tight. Repeat for the rest of the row. Then, use scissors to trim the fringe so that the bottom is straight. If desired, add a knitting tag. Your scarf is complete!

# Rainbow Fingerless Gloves

**SIZING:**
Approximately
4" wide x 7.5" tall

These rainbow fingerless gloves will keep your hands warm—and a smile on your face, as the bright colors light up your cold winter days!

## Supplies

- [ ] 48 needle knitting machine
- [ ] Weight 4/Medium yarn
- [ ] Crochet hook
- [ ] Darning needle
- [ ] Scissors
- [ ] Knitting tag (optional)

## Quick Recipe

### GLOVES (KNIT 2):
- 48 needle circular knitting machine
- Cast on and off with scrap yarn

- Knit 5 rows in the scrap yarn
- Knit 7 rows of red
- Knit 6 rows of orange
- Knit 6 rows of yellow
- Knit 6 rows of green
- Knit 6 rows of blue
- Knit 7 rows of purple
- Knit 5 rows in the scrap yarn

### STEP 1: KNITTING THE PIECES
Cast on to a 48 needle circular knitting machine using scrap yarn. Knit 5 rows in the scrap yarn. Switch to the red, leaving a long tail to use later for seaming. **Knit 7 rows in red. Knit 6 rows in orange. Knit 6 rows in yellow. Knit 6 rows in green. Knit 6 rows in blue. Knit 7 rows in purple.** Switch back to the scrap yarn, leaving a long yarn tail in the purple. **Knit 5 rows in the scrap yarn.** Continue knitting until the work falls off the needles. Pull the work out of the machine and gently stretch out the stitches. Repeat the same process again, to knit the second glove.

### STEP 2: SECURE THE YARN TAILS
Turn the pieces inside out. Secure all the yarn tails from the colors changes with a few good knots and trim the tails. Turn the work right side out.

### STEP 3: SEAMING THE ENDS
Use a crochet hook to seam the ends closed on both pieces. (See pages 14-15 for details). Remove the scrap yarn.

### STEP 4: SEAMING THE GLOVES
The piece should measure approximately 7.5" tall. Thread the purple yarn tail onto a darning needle. Use the Mattress Stitch to seam the sides together. (See pages 22-23 for details). Seam until you reach halfway through the blue stripe. Tie a knot on the inside of the glove, and thread the yarn **through only one side of the glove** until you reach the end of the green stripe. Secure the yarn with another knot on the inside of the glove, and then continue seaming with the Mattress Stitch until the end of the glove. Pull the yarn fairly tightly as you work to create a clean seam.

Secure the yarn tails with a couple of good knots on the inside of the glove, and weave in and trim the ends.

Repeat the same process on the second glove.

### STEP 5: FINAL TOUCHES
If desired, add a knitting tag to the gloves. Your rainbow fingerless gloves are complete!

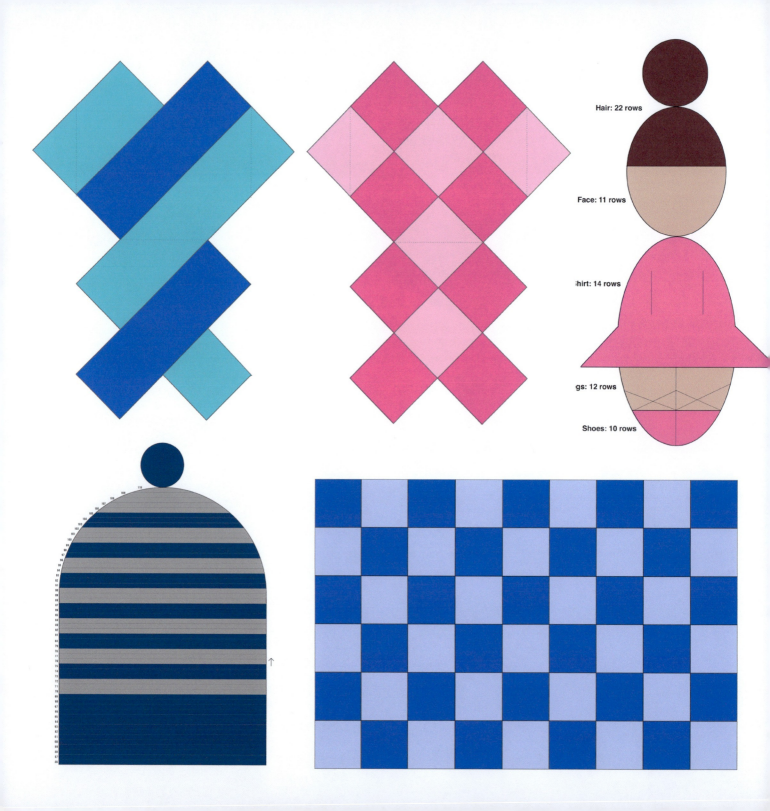

Hair: 22 rows

Face: 11 rows

Shirt: 14 rows

gs: 12 rows

Shoes: 10 rows

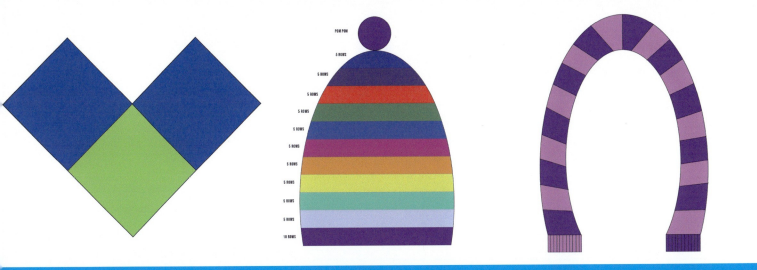

# The Templates

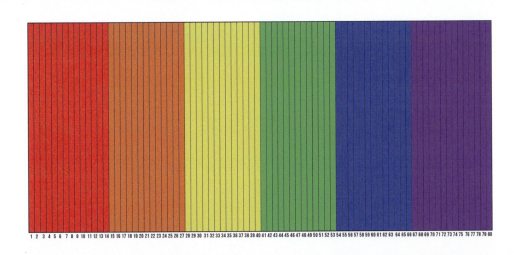

# Throw Pillows

Pattern: Pages 86-87

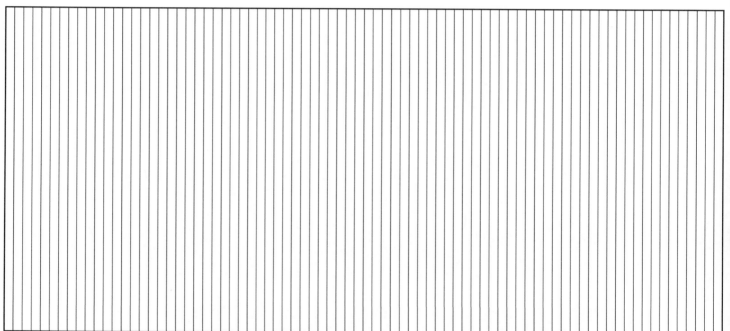

1 2 3 4 5 6 7 8 9 10 11 12 13 14 15 16 17 18 19 20 21 22 23 24 25 26 27 28 29 30 31 32 33 34 35 36 37 38 39 40 41 42 43 44 45 46 47 48 49 50 51 52 53 54 55 56 57 58 59 60 61 62 63 64 65 66 67 68 69 70 71 72 73 74 75 76 77 78 79 80

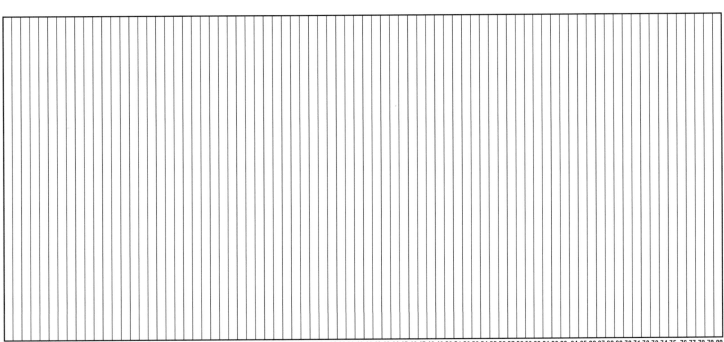

1 2 3 4 5 6 7 8 9 10 11 12 13 14 15 16 17 18 19 20 21 22 23 24 25 26 27 28 29 30 31 32 33 34 35 36 37 38 39 40 41 42 43 44 45 46 47 48 49 50 51 52 53 54 55 56 57 58 59 60 61 62 63 64 65 66 67 68 69 70 71 72 73 74 75 76 77 78 79 80

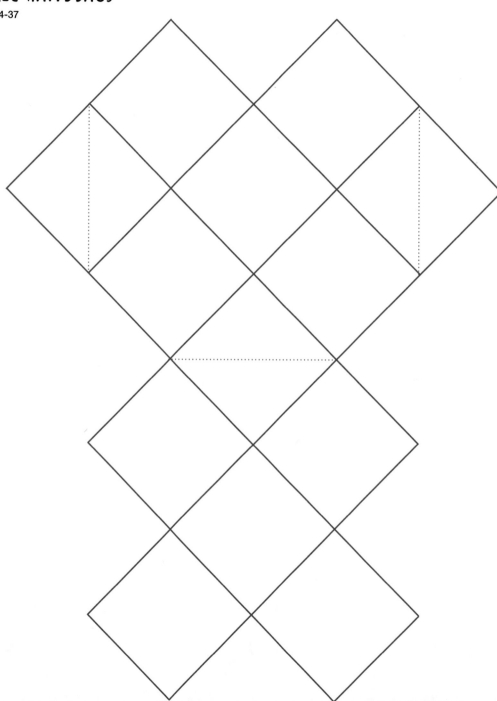

# Striped Handbags

Pattern: Pages 38-39

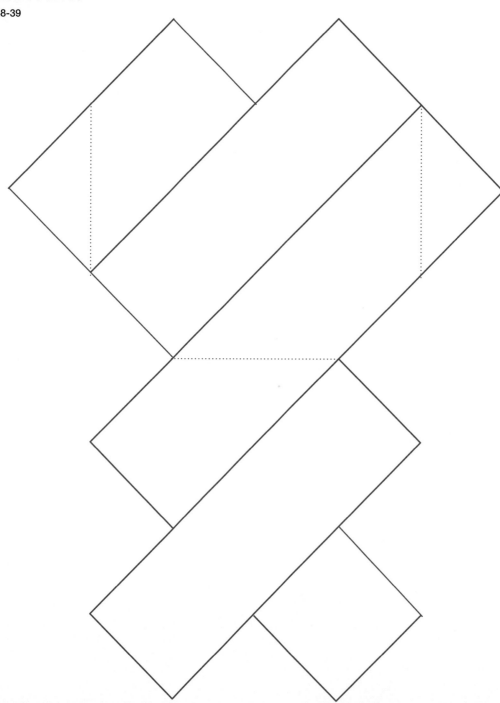

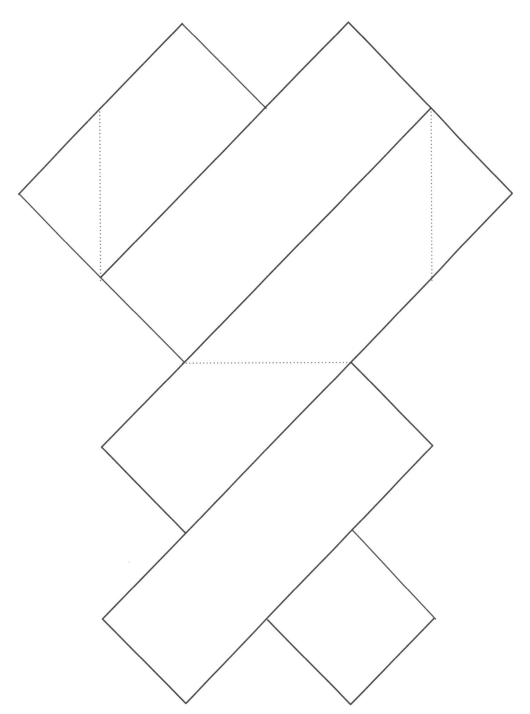

# Ballerina Dolls

Pattern: Pages 40-43

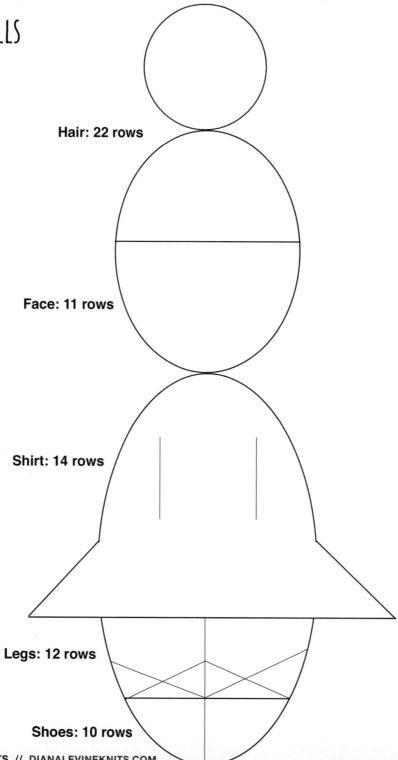

**Hair: 22 rows**

**Face: 11 rows**

**Shirt: 14 rows**

**Legs: 12 rows**

**Shoes: 10 rows**

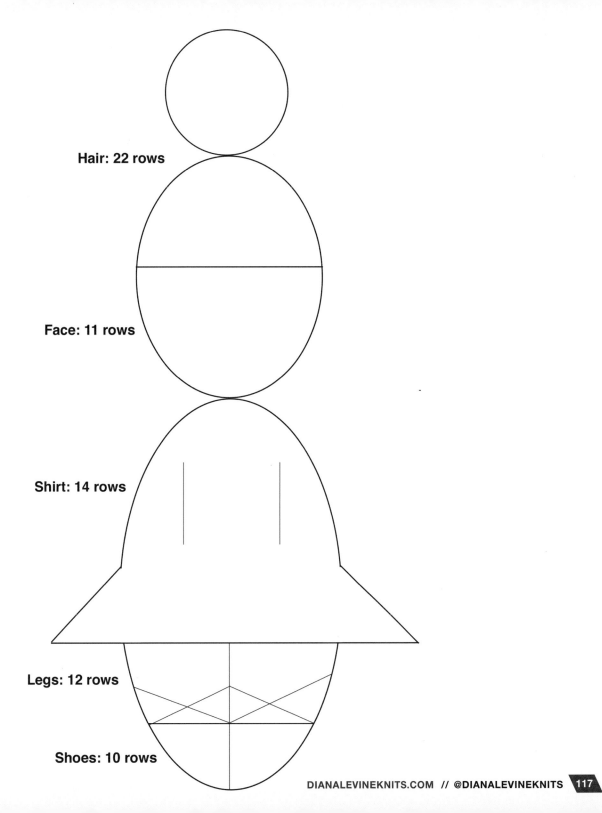

Hair: 22 rows

Face: 11 rows

Shirt: 14 rows

Legs: 12 rows

Shoes: 10 rows

# Checkered Blanket

Pattern: Pages 88-91

# Design-Your-Own-Hat Activity

Pattern: Pages 102-103

Knit 55 rows for the interior, and then follow the patttern from the bottom of the hat to the top.

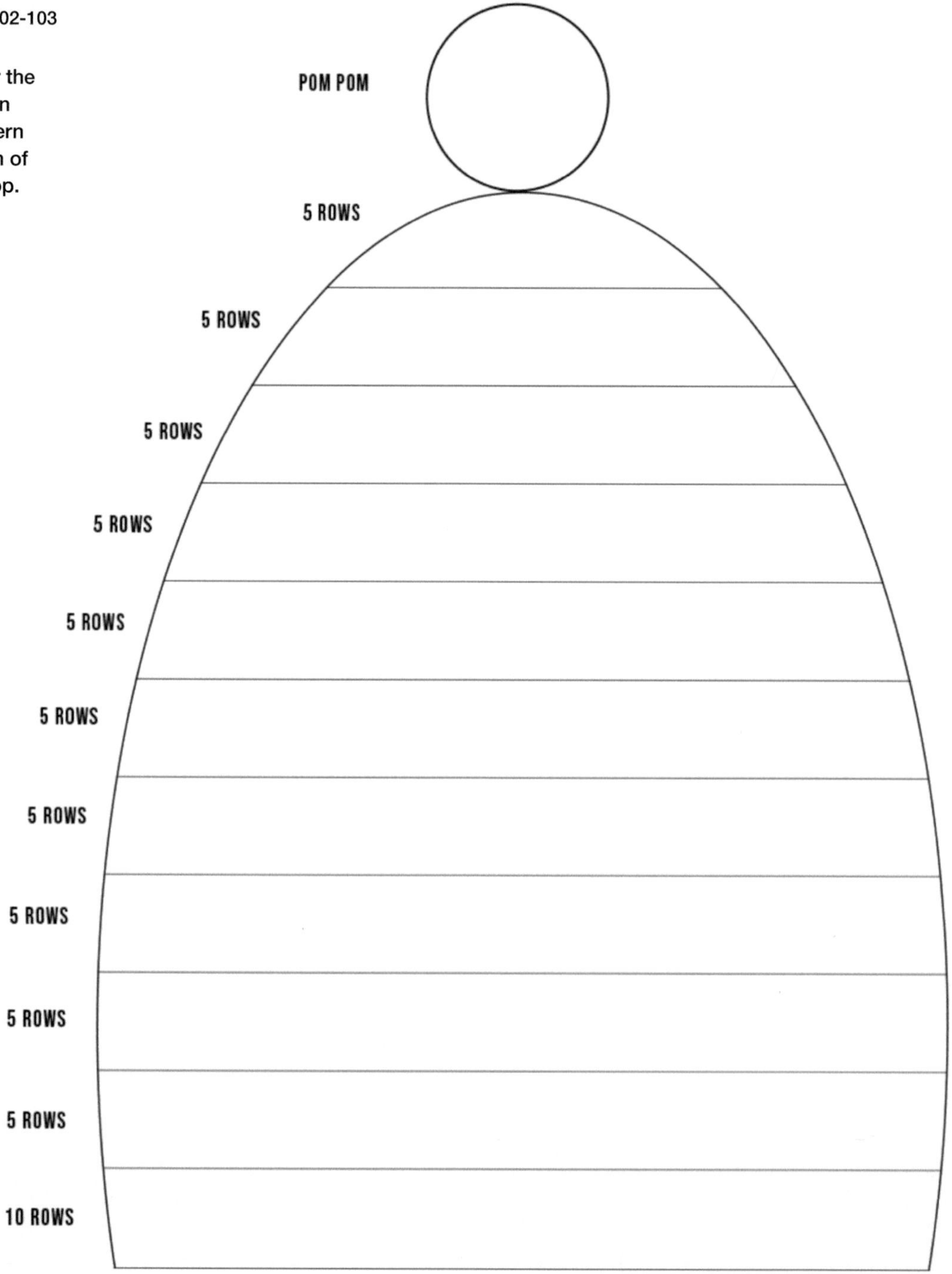

POM POM

5 ROWS

5 ROWS

5 ROWS

5 ROWS

5 ROWS

5 ROWS

5 ROWS

5 ROWS

5 ROWS

5 ROWS

5 ROWS

10 ROWS

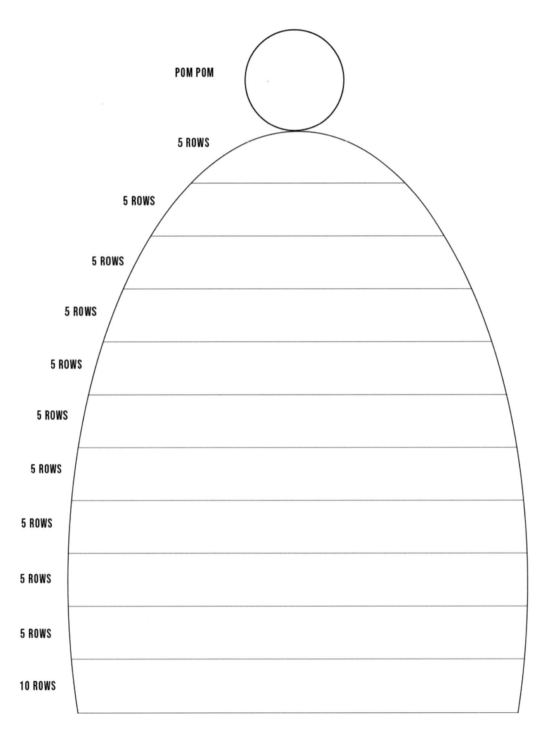

POM POM

5 ROWS

5 ROWS

5 ROWS

5 ROWS

5 ROWS

5 ROWS

5 ROWS

5 ROWS

5 ROWS

5 ROWS

5 ROWS

10 ROWS

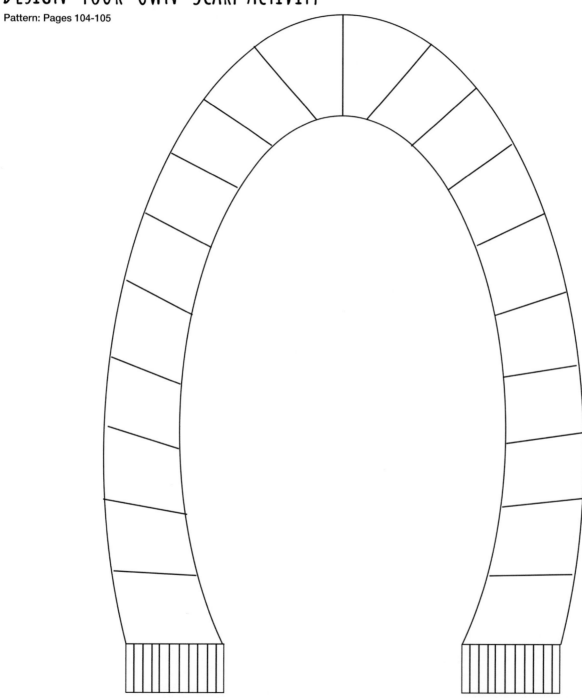

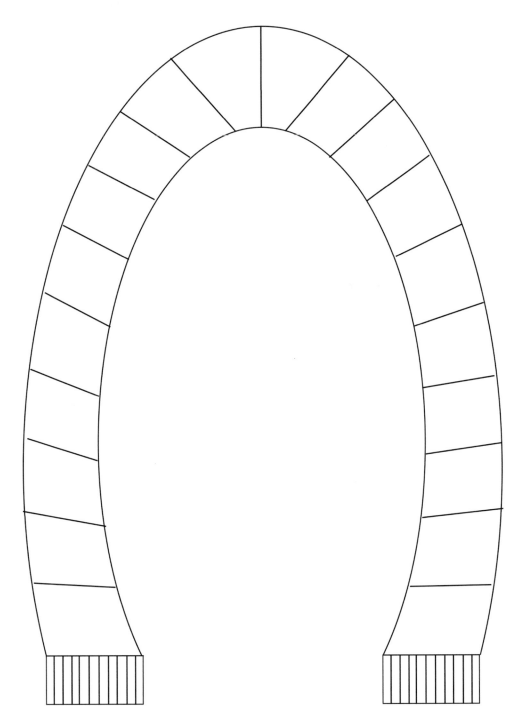

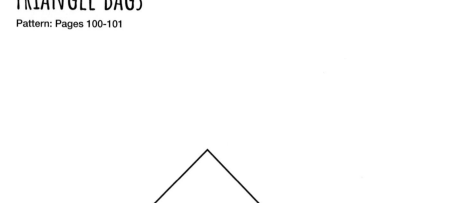

# Triangle Bags

Pattern: Pages 100-101

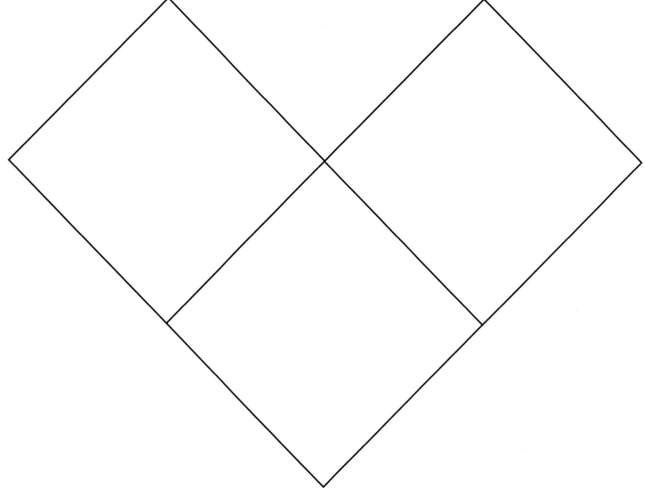

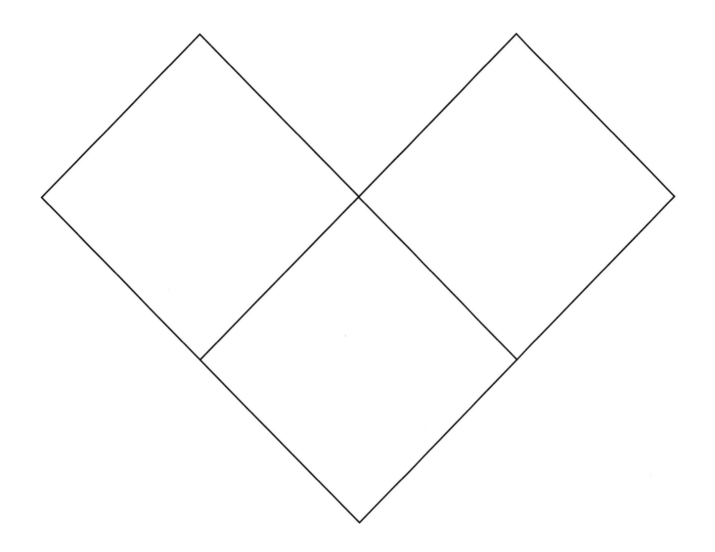

# Hat (Adult Sized, 46 or 48 needle machine)

Assembling a hat: Pages 28-29 | Follow the template from row 1 to row 110.

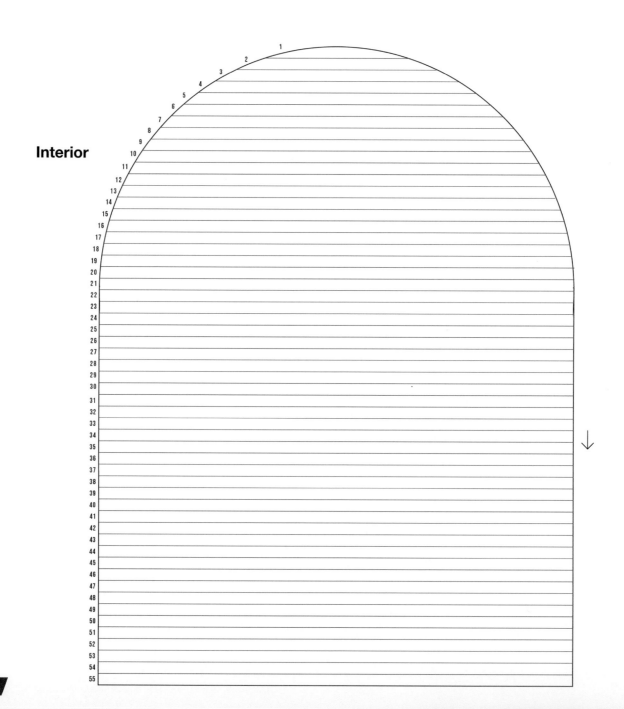

**Interior**

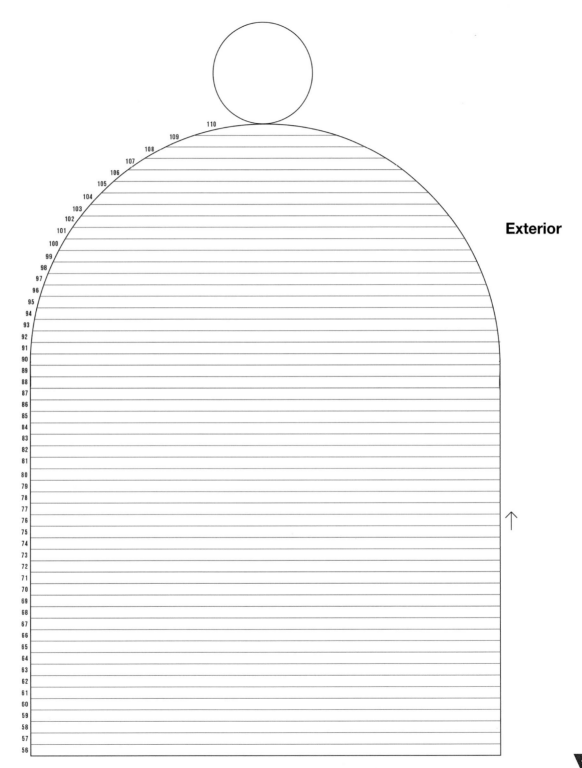

**Exterior**

# Hat (Adult Sized, 46 or 48 needle machine)

**Assembling a hat: Pages 28-29 | Follow the template from row 1 to row 110.**

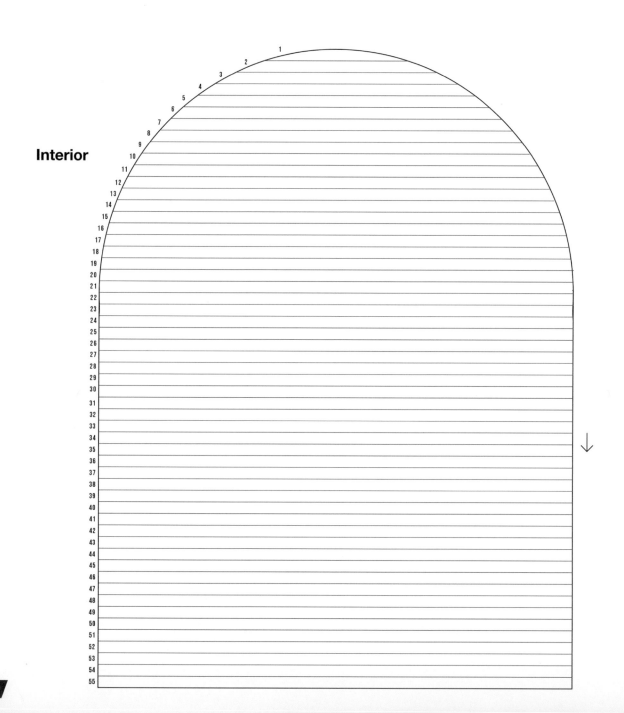

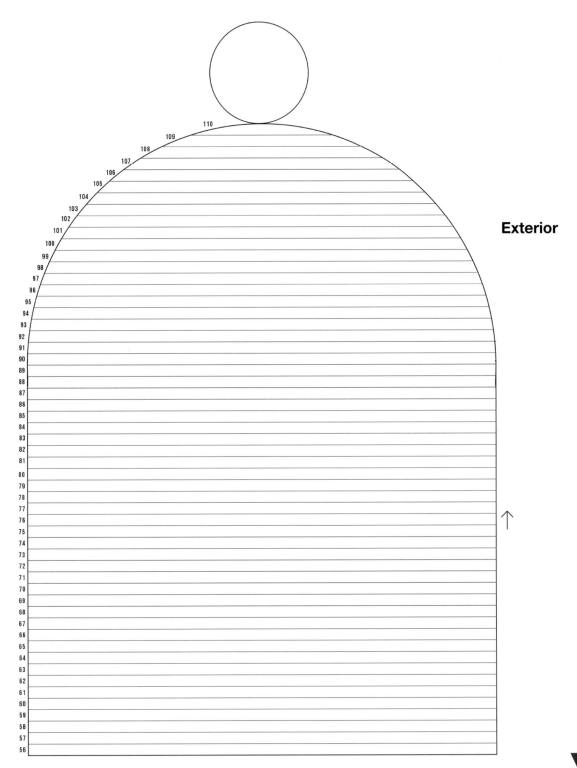

**Exterior**

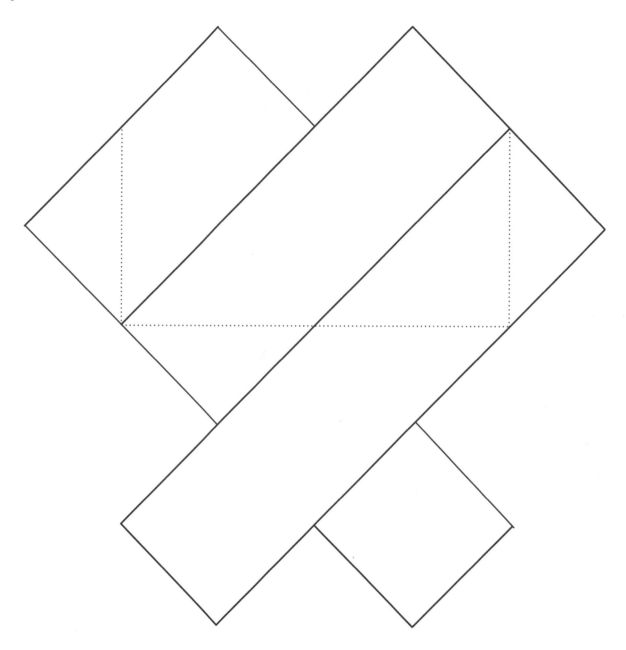

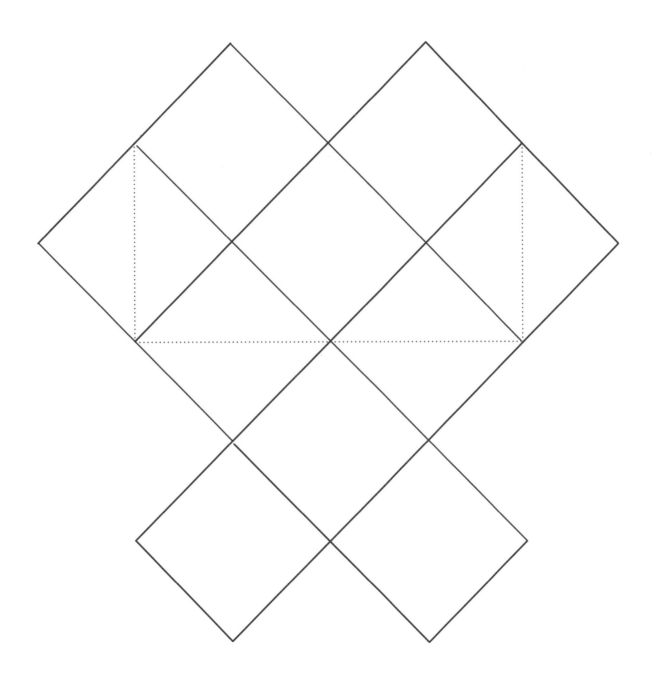

# Notes:

# Notes:

# My Knitting Machine Projects

Use this space to print photos of your final projects and tape them into the book. Or, use the blank spaces to sketch out ideas for your next designs and projects!

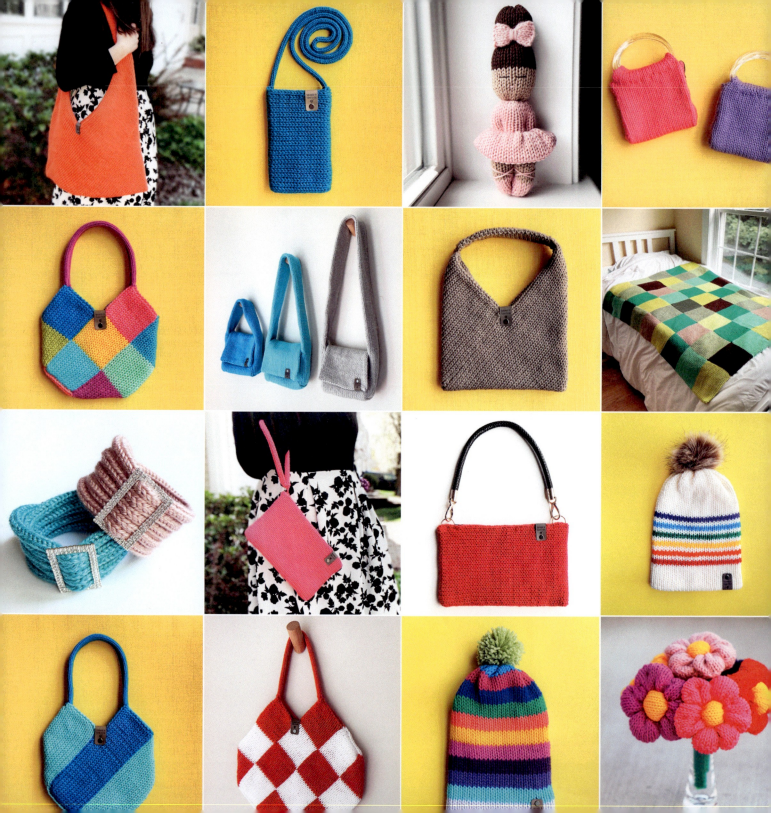